I, Grape
or
The Case for Fiction

I, Grape
or
The Case for
Fiction

ESSAYS

Brock Clarke

ACRE
CINCINNATI 2021

Acre Books is made possible by the support of the Robert and Adele Schiff Foundation and the Department of English at the University of Cincinnati.

ISBN-13 (pbk) 978-1-946724-36-6
ISBN-13 (ebook) 978-1-946724-37-3

The press is based at the University of Cincinnati, Department of English and Comparative Literature, McMicken Hall, Room 248, PO Box 210069, Cincinnati, OH, 45221–0069.

Acre Books books may be purchased at a discount for educational use. For information please email business@acre-books.com.

... my mother
had a bowl expressly shaped to
hold bananas, and simply
by putting grapes in it
I could get in trouble.

—MARY RUEFLE, "Sudden Additional Energy,"
   Trances of the Blast

Contents

I, Grape
or
The Case for Fiction

An Introduction, or Writing about What Matters Most

The world is too much for us, and we need help understanding it, and so no wonder we turn to the experts: the Paper of Record, *Morning Joe*, Breitbart, Barstool Sports, your cousin Terry's Twitter feed. As a writer, I of course turn to Literature, but since Literature isn't always up to the job (depending on what kind of Literature we read and what we think of as "the job"), I also turn to the regular email blasts of Penzeys Spices of Wauwatosa, Wisconsin, which regularly give you inside information about their latest deals on minced onion, but also, in a summer 2019 communique, right after telling you about their Mural of Flavor, let you know their feelings regarding the state of our union:

> [The mass shooting in] El Paso laid bare the truth of what the Republican Party and its supporters have become. And even

though I would, and have, told each of our children we don't use that word, it "sucks" that this time the Nazis we must face are our fellow citizens. But if history has been consistent in any message it's that you don't get to pick the Nazis you must face. It's time to be Americans once again.

But don't forget, *these new Onions* are freeze-dried and contain no anti-caking agents whatsoever.

Writers of email blasts about spices. Writers of fiction. We are all the same. All of us want to write about what matters most. But how? How do we do justice to the terrors, the injustices, the perils of the world, and also, how do we do that without being, you know, *boring*. Joy Williams identified this problem in an interview in *The Paris Review* in which Williams, an outspoken environmentalist (see her great book of essays *Ill Nature*), said, "I read a story recently about a woman who'd been on the lam and her husband dies and she ends up getting in her pickup and driving away at the end, and it was all about fracking, damage, dust to the communities, people selling out for fifty thousand dollars. It was so *boring*."

By *boring*, I think Williams meant predictable. And by *predictable*, I think I mean straightforward. This is not a new concern. For instance, Donald Barthelme identified it in his 1983 essay "Not-Knowing," in which he argued that "However much the writer might long to be, in his work, simple, honest, and straightforward, these virtues are no longer available to him. He discovers in being simple, honest, and straightforward, nothing much happens: he speaks the speakable, whereas what we are looking for is the as-yet unspeakable, the as-yet unspoken."

So, writers: speak the as-yet unspeakable, not the speakable. Excellent advice, but difficult to follow, especially in times of crisis, when the impulse is to be on topic. And in times of crisis, it is very easy to be on topic, there being so many problems that need to be urgently addressed, and so in our urgency we do what comes most easily: we address the problems directly, thus making what matters most to us seem lacking in nuance, lacking in surprise. Fiction writers are no less guilty of this than other writers, especially when allowed to write introductions like this one.

Fortunately, fiction writers, eventually, have to write fiction, so that we can justify calling ourselves fiction writers. And when we do write fiction, surprising things sometimes happen. That is one of the basic tenets of this book: when we write fiction, surprising things sometimes happen, especially when fiction writers take advantage of their chosen form's contrarian ability to surprise. There are dozens of examples of this—of the fiction writer's idiosyncratic imperative—in the pages that follow. But for now, as an example, we should briefly consider Colson Whitehead's work. Everyone knows about his Pulitzer Prize–winning novel *The Underground Railroad*, where escaped slaves are led to freedom by way of a literal underground railroad, thus providing cover, forty years after the fact, to ten-year-old boys like me who were mocked by classmates for insisting that the underground railroad was not a loose affiliation of people helping escaped slaves travel from the South to the North but was, you know, a real railroad that really operated underground. As great, though, and to my mind, maybe even greater, is Whitehead's first novel, *The Intuitionist*, a remarkable book about segregation, about the migration of African Americans from the rural South to the urban North, about passing, about minstrelsy, about tokenism, about the pressures and terrors of being one of the few Black people in mostly white institutions—a book that dramatizes these important subjects by way of a story about warring factions of elevator inspectors: the empiricists, who deal with facts and figures, and the intuitionists, who inspect elevators by using, well, their intuition. I taught this novel a few years ago, and before reading it, a student asked me what it was about. When I was done telling her what I just told you, the student screwed up her face and asked, "Why?" And that made me so happy. Because that's what fiction can do: it can take a subject we think we know, a subject that has been talked and written about, and it can make us ask "Why?" Which is why we read the book: to find out.

So, luckily, we have novelists like Whitehead. And also luckily, we have Penzeys of Wauwatosa, Wisconsin:

> Cumin is pretty much the now spice as we embrace the amazing flavors the last couple of generations of immigrants have brought to our door. For just $2, if you haven't already, why not welcome it in and give it a seat at your table? Grab a few to share.
>
> **And Hope.** These last few weeks have been some of the toughest of an historically tough last few years.

And that, my friends, is how it's done: you begin with cumin, and end up with hope. How did we get to this place? And where do we go from here? Well, yes, those are the big questions, and they are why we read fiction, and the latest from Penzeys, and why I hope you'll read this book, too: to find the surprising answers.

Speaking of this book, it came to exist not, at first, as a book but as a series of attempts over the last twenty years to figure out why we read fiction, and also as a series of attempts to convince people to read and love the kind of fiction that I read and love, and that I return to, obsessively, instead of the kind of fiction that I do not love, which I also return to, obsessively. Muriel Spark, Joy Williams, Donald Barthelme, Flannery O'Connor, Paul Beatty, George Saunders, Marilynne Robinson, John Cheever, Whitehead: these writers (and many others) appear in *I, Grape; or The Case for Fiction*. And sometimes they appear again. And then again. But so do my parents, and my children, and my grandmother, and my friends, and my students, and the city of Cincinnati, and the city of Little Falls, New York. Books, sometimes, have made me feel less alone. Just as often, they have made me feel my loneliness more acutely than I ever had before, or ever wanted to. The people and places in this book, likewise. Is it any wonder I'm obsessed with them? That I return to them? Is it any wonder I want you to turn to them, and then return to them, too?

What Can Fiction Do?
Not Much, Unless It's Set
in Cincinnati

I once knew a guy—a guy past the age where he could get away with tight jeans but who was still wearing them, a guy with not enough hair in front to justify the ponytail in back—who asked a friend of mine for a date. She was flustered by this, maybe because he was asking her out while I was standing right there next to her, and also maybe because she'd thought the guy was gay, and as everyone knows, when you're most flustered you're also most likely to tell the truth, which was why my friend blurted out, "I thought you were gay."

"What?" the guy said, obviously unnerved, but trying to compose himself, stroking his ponytail, tugging at his jeans. "Why would you think that?"

"I don't know," my friend said, obviously embarrassed and wanting to end of the conversation. "I just thought you were gay, that's all."

"Well, I'm not," the guy said.

"Okay," she said. "I believe you."

"Good," the guy said. Then, trying to make sure my friend really did believe him, he said something he shouldn't have: "I'm *very* heterosexual."

Is there a weaker, sadder, more futile word in the English language than *very*? Is there another word as fully guaranteed to prove the opposite of what its speaker or writer intends it to prove? Is there another word that so clearly states, on the speaker's or writer's behalf, "I'm not going to even *try* to find right word" or "No matter how hard I try, I'm not going to find the right word"? Is there a less specific, less helpful, less necessary, less potent word in our vocabulary? There is not. The weatherman knows this when he tells us to bundle up because it's going to be *very* cold outside. The mother knows this when she tells her teenagers, whom she's caught smoking out behind the garage again, that she's *very* disappointed in them. Elmer Fudd knows this when he tells Bugs Bunny to be *vewy* quiet. My students know this when they write, in their stories and by way of providing their characters with physical details I tell them their characters need in order to be characters, that so-and-so is *very* heavy, or *very* beautiful, or *very* statuesque. We all know this is an awful, lame word (John Cheever, who in his story "The Wrysons" describes a group of rich people who sail up and down the Eastern Seaboard as being "*very* aquatic," manages to employ (or deploy) the word as he did others—knowingly, beautifully; but it's dicey to try to write like Cheever, as I know very well, and maybe Cheever himself did, too). So why do we use this awful, lame word? Is it because we're too lazy to find the right word to describe the things that are important to us? Or is it impossible to find the right word to describe those important things? When we say *very*, do we say, "I don't care"? Or do we say, "I care too much"?

I was watching my older son read a book the other day—it was *The Clue of the Screeching Owl*, volume 41 in the Hardy Boys series. He was sitting on his bed, the book in front of his face, and didn't notice me in the doorway. I must have stood there for five minutes, watching him read, watching him and watching him and falling deeper and deeper in love. What is it about seeing your children read that makes you love them so much, love them as much as you should love them all the time? I don't think it's only writers who feel this way. I don't think it's only readers who feel this way, either. I don't even think it has anything to do with reading—after all, as far as spectator sports go, watching someone read a book is only slightly more exciting than watching someone play golf. Maybe it's easier to love a child at rest than a child in motion. Or maybe to watch a child reading is to watch a child not in any danger, a child you haven't put in peril, a child you haven't screwed up, or screwed up yet, or screwed up totally. Or maybe to watch a child who is unaware of you watching them is to watch something so perfect and unselfconscious that it is impossible do anything but love them.

"What?" my son said. Because of course he'd noticed me standing there, and was now reading me the way he'd been reading the book a moment earlier, except he was reading me skeptically, suspecting, maybe, that I wanted something from him, whereas he'd been reading *The Clue of the Screeching Owl* with pleasure, and this, by the way, is the main reason we read: the people we love always want something from us—namely, they want us to love them back, whether they deserve it or not; books want us to love them, too, and if they deserve it and we do love them, then great; but if they do not deserve it and we do not love them, then there is nothing that books can do to punish us. Books are feeble. This is just one of this essay's many inspirational lessons.

Anyway, my older son noticed me standing in the doorway and said, "What?" "Nothing," I said. Because how could I tell him how I felt? How could I tell him that I worry about him every second of every day except when he is reading? How could I tell him that I would die if something bad happened to him, even something just a little bad that only caused me to die a little bit, and so as long as he kept reading and let me watch him do it, I wouldn't have to die yet? How could I tell him that by reading he was giving me more time to love him? How do you say this kind of stuff to your son, or to anyone else, for that matter? You don't; I didn't. Instead I said, "I love you very much."

My son looked at me over the top of his book. It was that parental look, full of disappointment. "*Very?*" his look seemed to say. "Is that the best you can do?" And then he returned to his book, which, presumably, hopefully, would do better.

But it did not do better. This is the point toward which I've been meandering. The Hardy Boys and their case did not do better. They could not do better. They will never do better. This is another of this essay's inspirational lessons: one should never go looking for uplift, or wisdom, or greatness, or transcendence, in any of the Hardy Boys books. You will not find those things in those places. This has long been the basic, vulgar, foundational premise of our little creative writing corner of higher education: do not read shit. It is perfectly acceptable, on the other hand, to watch shit on television or at the movies. This is absolutely allowed, even encouraged—think of the watching of shit on television and at the theater as a kind of perpetual rumspringa for fiction writers—but whatever you do, do not read shit. Reading shit is bad for you. Instead, spend your time learning to appreciate and understand great literature. Great literature will make you write and feel better, even if it sometimes makes you write and feel worse, too. The other day, a colleague and I were complaining about our bad head colds, and she shared with me her secret Canadian home remedy: whenever she feels a cold coming on, my colleague makes and then chugs a brew that is half apple cider and half vinegar. My colleague must have recognized the look of pre-puke horror on my face when she told me this, because she then said, "I know, I know. But if you can handle it at first, then later on you'll be much better off." If there is a better metaphor for how many of us learn to love difficult works of literary fiction, then I don't want to know what it is.

Yet another inspirational lesson: reading literary fiction is not dissimilar to drinking vinegar to rid yourself of mucus. Which is good. Because the opposite—not reading literary fiction but trying to write fiction anyways—is much, much worse. If you're ever in doubt of this, then you should try teaching an introductory fiction writing class. A few years ago, for instance, a student of mine in one such class handed in a caveperson story—the kind of story in which the characters' names all end with *or* (Tor, Zor, Exor) and where the men spend their twenty pages fending off the attacks of saber-toothed tigers and the women spend their twenty pages in their caves, teaching their children to speak monosyllabically and warning them to stay away from fire, since they don't know whether they've invented the fire or if it's a gift from one of their gods and which, in any case, isn't keeping them anywhere near warm, maybe because it's winter— it's always winter—and they're dressed in saber-toothed tiger-skin bikinis and loincloths, which is, of course, why the saber-toothed tigers are attacking them in the first place. In my student's story, the tigers successfully devoured the women and children, because their cavemen had, improbably and anachronistically, figured out how to construct a still from native materials and then make liquor—a process that included some sort of leafy plant with a high alcohol content, a long piece of rubber tubing coiled like a bedspring, and a large pot that, my student's omniscient narrator informed us, was the kind of thing you might use to boil a lobster—and so were passed out drunk and unable to save their prehistoric dependents.

This kind of story, by the way, is why we tell our beginning fiction-writing students to write what they know, and why we also tell them that one has to learn the rules of fiction writing before one goes about breaking them. These pieces of advice are yet more feebleness. The first is feeble because, after all, our students don't know very much, and we know they don't very much because we were their age and knew just as little, which was why we actually listened to our fiction-writing teachers when they told us, feebly, to write what we know. The second piece of advice—about knowing the rules before breaking them—is even more feeble and again in an especially parental way, like a father telling his son that he has to learn how to drive the car before he goes out and wrecks it.

Even so, after reading a twenty-page story in which Cor—who can't make a decent fire or loincloth but *is* clever enough to invent the distillery—ends up doing shots of homemade Everclear and then passes out in his own vomit while a fanged big cat has its blood-thirsty way with his family, you're ready to do anything, including give your students what you know is feeble advice, and I would have done just that, except another student in that class handed in a western in which someone brave and good with a big hat rides that horse and shoots that gun, and another handed in a science fiction story full of silver jumpsuits and hovercrafts, and another handed in a horror story featuring a tooth fetishist with his dank cellar and his knockout gas and pliers, and so on, and I thought what any of you would have thought, which was: What the hell is going on here? Where are they getting this stuff? They weren't getting it from me—I was teaching them literary short fiction, which is what I believed and still do believe is what they should be reading and learning— and that's when I realized that telling my students to write what they knew would have been especially feeble, because they were already doing it, and what they knew was science fiction, the western, *Clan of the Cave Bear*.

It seemed to me that, as their teacher, I had two options: one, I could tell them that what they knew was all wrong and to go out and know something else; or, two, I could tell them that if they were hell bent on knowing, say, cavepeople fiction, then they should read George Saunders's "Pastoralia," a novella about a man and a woman playing a cavecouple in a theme park. So I told my student to read "Pastoralia" and then rewrite her story with the novella in mind. She didn't a change a thing, except for the moment when one of the cavechildren yells something at one of the other cavechildren and his mother whispers at him to, quote, "Use your *cave* voice." True, the tiger still ate them, but at least it was a somewhat more satisfying meal.

And I wonder if this—the making of a somewhat more satisfying meal—is the best any of us can ever do and should ever want to do. Joy Williams argues that "A writer starts out . . . wanting to be a transfiguring agent, and ends up usually just making contact with other human beings." To put it more prosaically, writers aspire to make something great, but perhaps we'd be better off aspiring to just make a somewhat more satisfying meal. Or even an awful meal. A meal that tastes even worse than my colleague's vinegary cold cure. A meal so terrible that, if I abandoned the analogy and turned the meal into a novel again, the novel would not be allowed to appear in print form, not even in a Kindle or NOOK, a novel so terrible that only a blind, widowed grandmother would want to listen to it.

I'm speaking, of course, of my own grandmother, who began listening to books on tape after she'd gone blind. Not completely blind—she was the kind of sweet, macularly degenerated old woman who walked carefully with the help of a tri-pronged cane while wearing the kind of enormous wraparound shades that might be also be useful if you needed to weld something—but blind enough so that around age eighty-five she was forced to make the switch from regular-sized print books to large-print books, until eventually she couldn't read even those, which was when she started listening to books on tape.

My grandmother, who is dead now, got her books on tape from the Association for the Blind and Visually Impaired, which my grandmother called simply "the blind." As in, "When are the blind going to bring me some new books?" This would drive my father and my aunt bananas: the blind, they'd explain, did not bring the books; the *Association for the Blind* did. But that didn't stop my grandmother from calling them "the blind." Maybe she liked the image of a blind person driving a car, leaning over the passenger seat, rolling down and then reaching through the window, opening the mailbox, retrieving or depositing a book on tape, and then driving off. Or maybe she liked driving her children bananas. In either case, this is just one of the reasons I miss her so much.

Anyway, my grandmother got the tapes from the blind, and she listened to them in her bedroom, in her house in Connecticut. It'd also been my grandfather's bedroom, and house, until he died in 1993. I know this sounds lonely—an old widow, lying in her room, with her eyes closed, listening to her books on tape—and it was lonely. At least, it seemed that way to me when I stood in the hallway outside her door and eavesdropped. The books were usually terrible, moderately filthy romance novels that favored words like "throbbing" (the blind's lending library was limited in those days; I know it's better now). I should have felt ashamed to stand in the hallway eavesdropping on my grandmother. But I wasn't ashamed. I did not think, "I really shouldn't be doing this." Instead I thought, "How can she listen to this crap?" My grandmother rarely complained about these books, but to me it seemed like the saddest thing: that in a world full of great books, my grandmother was reduced to listening to *this*. I remember one day in particular, when I was supposed to drive my grandmother to the cemetery where my grandfather is buried. She was in her bedroom, listening to this breathless exchange from her book on tape:

"I want you," said the man.

"That is what I want, too," said the woman.

Then I knocked on the door. The tape player clicked off. The door was closed, but I'd seen my grandmother get out of bed enough times to be able to picture it. I could picture her swiveling her body until she was in a sitting position and her blue Keds were resting on the floor. I could picture her leaving them on the floor for a beat or two, as though making sure her feet and the floor knew what they expected of each other. I could picture her rising slowly, with one hand still on the bed, just in case. I could picture her other hand reaching for the cane. Then, a second later, the door opened, and there was my grandmother wearing her dark glasses. "I'm ready," she said.

We made our slow way to the car, and then I drove her to the cemetery. We got out of the car. I stood next to my grandmother as she leaned over, placed her hand on the top of my grandfather's headstone, and said, "Hi, love."

And then I started crying. My grandmother heard me; she looked up and gave me a slight nod, as if to say, *I know*. Which made me cry even harder. What my grandmother had said was so genuine, and beautiful, and it made me miss my grandfather so much, and it made me realize how much she missed him, too, and I would have done anything not to have heard it. I would have done anything to be back in the house, listening to the book on tape with its lousy dialogue and its cheap longing. Because it is harder to feel real longing when you're listening to cheap longing, which is maybe why my grandmother needed to listen to those books on tape, and why I now need to think about her listening to them, too.

Behold this essay's third-to-last inspirational lesson: it is harder to feel real longing when you're listening to cheap longing. The standard response from our little creative writing corner of higher education would be that cheapness is the enemy, that by definition and in point of fact cheapness is unsatisfying and enervating and ephemeral and unsustaining, and we should not only *allow* ourselves to feel real longing but we should *make* ourselves feel real longing; we should *want* to feel real longing. But why in the hell would anyone want *that*? Wouldn't any thinking person want to feel anything *but* that? T. S. Eliot has been widely criticized for claiming in "Tradition and the Individual Talent" that "Poetry is not a turning loose of emotion, but an escape from emotion; it is not the expression of personality, but an escape from personality." But in zeroing in on this sentence, we often ignore the one that follows: "But of course, only those who have personality and emotions know what it means to want to escape from these things." Eliot is of course infamous for behaving like the Saint Peter of Western Literary Culture, but this last statement sounds to me less like literary gatekeeping and more like common goddamn sense.

Earlier, I suggested that we should not look for greatness, etc., in the Hardy Boys. This is an argument so uncontroversial as to be offensive. Of course Eliot would agree with it. What I think Eliot would balk at is extending the argument to say that one should not go looking for greatness in any book, of any era, especially our own, and especially not in one whose creator believes not only in the transcendence and greatness of art but believes their work has achieved transcendence and greatness, and also believes they have achieved these things by populating their book with people who believe they and their book have achieved these things. I'm thinking of one of the most acclaimed novels in recent memory, Joseph O'Neill's *Netherland,* a novel that is often compared to *The Great Gatsby* by people who presumably have not read *The Great Gatsby*, and who only know that it is about a bunch of rich people. *Netherland* is about a bunch of rich people. It's also about how living in New York City after 9/11 makes these rich people very *nervous,* and about how eventually fleeing New York City after 9/11 makes them feel very *guilty*. I confess to not being entirely charitable toward these people and their feelings. Perhaps because of how they're presented early in the novel, when the narrator, a Dutch banker named Hans, and his English wife Rachel, drive past a park hosting several cricket matches. Rachel calls Hans's attention to the scene by saying, "Oh! Look, darling," and Hans then narrates, "From our elevated vantage point the scene—Van Cortlandt Park on a Sunday—appeared as a cheerful pell-mell, and as we drove by Rachel said, 'It looks like a Brueghel,' and I smiled at her because she was exactly right, and as I remember I put my hand on her stomach. It was July 1999. She was seven months pregnant with our son."

This is fiction as cultural self-congratulation. It's as though the Metropolitan Museum of Art has knocked up Choate Rosemary Hall, who in two months will give birth to a child named Impeccable Taste. Soon after in the novel, Choate Rosemary Hall moves to London with Impeccable Taste while poor Metropolitan Museum of Art has to shack up in the Chelsea Hotel, where he longs for his family, until he finally indulges his longing and also moves to London, and then he and Choate Rosemary Hall go on a very expensive vacation where they indulge in some more very expensive, very tasteful longing.

Now might be a good time ask: What is my problem? Is this not exactly the kind of novel we should want? A novel that takes as its inspiration and aspiration not the Hardy Boys and cavepeople but High Art and its attendant Eternal Verities, a novel that clearly knows the difference between cheap longing and genuine longing and comes down squarely on the side of the latter? It is. This is the book for which we've been longing, myself included. But should I have been longing for something else? Because as it turned out, as I read and reread *Netherland* I longed for it to be a much different novel, a novel in which Hans's pregnant wife Rachel has left him because he won't stop putting his hand on her pregnant stomach, and she's told him a thousand times, *Wow, Hans, I really do not like it when you put your hand on my pregnant stomach the way you do. It's not comforting, it's creepy, so please stop it,* and yet he does not stop it, he keeps placing his hand on Rachel's stomach, until one day she says, *I swear to fucking God, Hans . . .* but she doesn't get to finish the sentence, because he interrupts her and says, *What's the matter, darling?* and then he *does it again*—and so she leaves him and moves not to London but to Cincinnati, wherever that is, where she meets and kind of falls in love with a middle-school guidance counselor, whatever that is, a guidance counselor who wears too tight jeans and a ponytail, and she and Hans's daughter move in with the guidance counselor and after a few years Hans moves to Cincinnati as well, so that he can be closer to his daughter and also because he fears that the guidance counselor is allowing and maybe even encouraging his daughter, whose name is Pam, to read books like *Clan of the Cave Bear,* and because the Eternal Verities don't contribute much toward Hans's rent in Cincinnati, he ends up getting a job in research and development at Proctor and Gamble, and when he's not laboring mightily to revive the Pringles brand he writes a blog, a blog among other blogs, a blog that no one ever reads, a blog entitled an Exiled King in the Queen City, a blog that is devoted to New York and how Hans can't stop longing for it.

I might have just made it seem as though I believe Mr. O'Neill's novel *Netherland* would be better if it had ended up being set in Cincinnati. What I meant to say is that I believe that all novels, including my own, would be better if they ended up being set in Cincinnati.

In 2010, just after I moved away from Cincinnati, I met a nice, smart, worldly woman—she had lived in New York City, and Los

Angeles, and Paris, and now she lived, like me, in Portland, Maine. When I told her I had just moved from Cincinnati, she said, "Oh, good for you!" And then, because she was not dumb like a caveperson or blind like my grandmother, she could see that she might have offended me, and so she said, "I mean, right?"

This is why every novel would be better if it were set in Cincinnati: because no one knows what happens there. I do not mean that Cincinnati is a blank slate. We should always distrust writers who refer to real places in the world as being blank slates. These are writers who have just taken a lot of OxyContin, and they are the same writers who, right *before* they take a lot of OxyContin, like to talk about how their characters have taken over their novels. Cincinnati is not a blank slate. If anything, it is a broken slate, and there's some brown grass sticking up in the cracks. But let's not talk about slate anymore. Let's go back to the worldly woman who doesn't know anything about Cincinnati, which isn't entirely correct: she knows that she has not lived there and that she has never longed to live there and she knows that she has lived in other places and that they are important, great places, places other people have longed to live, places we know a lot about, places about which we have already kind of made up our minds when it comes to the subject of their greatness, their worthiness as the objects of our longing, and once people have actually satisfied their longing and lived in those places, that means they have won. And when someone wins, that means someone else must lose. That's what the worldly woman knew about Cincinnati: that it had lost. That it was the city of losers. The band Steely Dan sings, "We've got a name for the winners in the world. I want a name when I lose." The name for when you lose is Cincinnati. That is why all novels should be set there.

Let me tell you a little bit about Cincinnati. I lived there for nine years. My house looked out on a Catholic elementary school parking lot. Often, when I should have been working or something, I sat on my front porch and smoked cigarettes and watched the students run around during gym class or recess and hurl balls at each other. The students seemed like something out of the past: they wore the same uniforms (light blue shirts and dark blue pants for the boys; plaid dresses for the girls) my classmates and I wore in Catholic elementary school thirty-five years ago. The balls they chucked at each other were the same, too—hard, oversized rubber things that were more *thud* than *boing*, balls that other schools in other places had probably banned, or gotten rid of, or given away to Catholic elementary schools in Cincinnati. I couldn't believe schoolchildren were allowed to throw things like that at each other anymore. But they were, and did. One day, when I was smoking and watching, a boy ran up holding a ball that was much bigger than a watermelon and probably just as soft. When he was within, oh, a foot of his equally pint-sized victim, the boy threw the ball as hard as he could at the back of the other boy's head. The struck boy didn't fall, but he did stagger around a lot, and I bet he was at least a little bit concussed. Anyway, finally he stopped staggering, turned around and yelled at his attacker, "You dink!"

Mark Twain is supposed to have said, "When the end of the world comes, I want to be in Cincinnati because it's always twenty years behind the times." To put it another way: before I moved to Cincinnati, I hadn't heard anyone say *dink* since I was in Catholic elementary school myself; but in the space of a few weeks after I'd moved to Cincinnati in the summer of 2001, I heard the word used twice. The first was a bar called the Barrelhouse, where I'd gone to see a band called the Ass Ponys. The Ass Ponys' most recent (and last) album, *Lohio*, had just been enthusiastically reviewed in *Village Voice*. Or maybe it was *Rolling Stone*. Anyway, I'd read the review. So had lots of other people. The bar was full. You could tell it wasn't full very often, because it was hard to get a drink. People were buying several beers at a time, just so they wouldn't have to bother later on. I bought three beers and then had a difficult time figuring out how I was supposed to hold them, so I drank the first one really quickly and put the empty glass on the bar. Then I only had to hold two beers, which was more manageable, but still pretty pathetic. I was by myself. I couldn't really understand how I'd ended up in Cincinnati. Like many of you, and like Hans and Rachel, as long as I'd been longing I'd been longing to live in the center of the universe. And yet here I was in Cincinnati, a place I'd never even thought of before I moved there, a place I was surprised to learn was next to Kentucky and Indiana, two other places I'd never thought of. Plus, only three months before the concert there had been race riots in the city. A white cop had shot and killed an unarmed Black man, the latest in a series of white cops shooting unarmed Black men, and afterward a lot of buildings were burned, a lot of windows were broken, and a lot of people were hurt. A city like Cincinnati never makes the national news for anything good, and sure enough the tv showed repeated shots of groups of Black men knocking stuff over and setting fire to already abandoned buildings and throwing rocks and bricks at mostly white riot police with their shields and helmets. The Barrelhouse itself was in the neighborhood where the man had been killed, the neighborhood that had been most wrecked by the riots. I had never lived in a place where such terrible things had happened. But then, as Mr. O'Neill's novel reminds us (if we needed reminding), 9/11 happened and changed everything forever, and one of the ways it did that is by making most people forget about the riots in Cincinnati, if they ever knew about them in the first place, and by making others wonder how significant the riots really were compared to The Big Terrible. It was extremely disorienting. I remember standing in the Barrelhouse with my two beers and thinking, Where in the hell am I? And why hasn't the concert started yet? Because the concert hadn't started yet, although the band was on stage, messing around with their instruments. Their lead singer and rhythm guitarist, Chuck Cleaver, looked like a guy that a high school football coach could never convince to try out for the team: he had thick, tattooed forearms and a biggish belly and graying wiry hair and a goatee that was long and wide and wild enough that it deserved to be considered a beard. The bassist, Randy Cheek (those really were their names: Chuck Cleaver and Randy Cheek), was short, and unbelievably white, and wore unbelievably dorky thick black glasses; his hair shot up from the top of his hairline, which was high, and his jeans were rolled up many times and still were too long. He was smoking; he looked like he'd always smoked; he looked like he'd grown up smoking in a cave. The guitarist, Bill Alletzhauser, was also short, but handsomer, and younger-looking than the rest of the band. While his bandmates tuned their instruments, Alletzhauser kept looking around the bar, as though searching for another band to rescue him. The drummer, Dave Morrison, was the tallest drummer I'd ever seen; he was the tallest person I'd ever seen who wasn't a basketball player. Toward the back of the stage, sitting behind his drums, his knees up to his chest, he looked about as comfortable as a big man wedged into a small airplane seat. There were other bands from southwestern Ohio at this point in history who'd made it somewhat big in the indie rock world. Cincinnati's Afghan Whigs, for instance, who reeked of sex; Dayton's Guided by Voices, who reeked of booze. But it was hard to tell what the Ass Ponys reeked of. They didn't look exactly like a band, but they didn't look exactly like anything else, either.

This description also holds true for a novel set in Cincinnati: it doesn't exactly look like a novel, but it doesn't exactly look like anything else, either.

Anyway, it was taking the band too long to tune their instruments. The band realized that and seemed to be laughing about what screw-ups they were. Finally, Chuck Cleaver stopped twisting the knobs on his guitar, then leaned into his mic and said. "I know what you're thinking. 'What a bunch of dinks.'"

Dinks! I thought, and might have actually said it out loud. It made me so happy to hear that long lost word! It was the sort of moment where you don't realize how much you've missed something until it immediately makes you so happy to have it back in your life again. But it could just have easily made me feel pathetic and sad and lonely, to be taking such pleasure in hearing and actually saying out loud this ridiculous, obsolete, childish word to myself, in a bar full of people I didn't know, drinking too many beers at one time. And this is exactly how I felt about my entire nine years in that great, grim city. I've never felt as happy and at home as I did when I lived in Cincinnati, except for those moments when I genuinely wanted to kill myself.

This, then, is Cincinnati (and this is also your novel set in Cincinnati): a place full of cigarette-smoking creeps who spy on schoolchildren as they brain each other on the playground, and race riots that were significant and terrible and life-changing and life-ending, but that not enough people paid attention to because the riots happened in Cincinnati, and because that same year something even more significant and terrible and life-changing and life-ending happened in the center of the universe. A city of too much drinking, a city populated by people who use the word *dink* and that's home to a band you've never heard of with the awful name Ass Ponys, which is only slightly less awful for being purposefully misspelled, but a band that is somehow great anyway. A city that makes you want to kill yourself when it isn't making you feel things you didn't know you could feel about things you didn't know you missed and that you should not have missed in the first place. This is why all novels would be better if they were set in Cincinnati, which is the name for when you lose. When you lose, when you are in Cincinnati, you are in a place of no assumed importance, where there is no point in distinguishing between high and low, between genuine longing and cheap longing; you are in a place where value always must be salvaged or jerry-rigged or struggled for. In other words, *earned*. A place where anything good ends up being surprising, because it would seem impossible. Even childhood. In John Cheever's "The Housebreaker of Shady Hill," the narrator asks this presumably rhetorical question: "Where were the trout streams of my youth, and other innocent pleasures?" But in your novel set in Cincinnati, the pleasures of your youth are not innocent; the pleasures are found in the degraded materials of youth; the pleasures are found in words like *dink,* or rather in using words like *dink* long after their expiration date.

Now, you might be thinking that I'm leaning awfully heavily on the word *dink,* which is, after all, such a shitty word. I agree: the word is shitty, and the world (at least the world of your novel set in Cincinnati) is also shitty, but the world is much less shitty than it might be because we have this perfect shitty word to help us describe how shitty it is.

This is this essay's penultimate inspirational lesson—the world is shitty, but the world is much less shitty than it might be because we have perfect shitty words to help us describe how shitty it is. The man who described himself as being very heterosexual and the woman who wrote the caveperson story and my almost blind grandmother knew this. I regret now my earlier mocking of them. When they were doing something worth mocking they were being from Cincinnati, but when I mocked them I was not.

You might know of three writers who, were they lawyers, would belong to the good-sounding law firm of Franzen, Chabon, and Lethem. Once in a while they write novels set in Cincinnati, and when they do I am jealous of them, just as I'm sometimes jealous of their fame, and their wealth, and their excellent heads of hair. But other times they write novels and stories and essays unironically and unself-deprecatingly championing the enduring virtues of Superman and Charlie Brown and the Hardy Boys, and when they do this they are not writing books set in Cincinnati because they are merely being nostalgic, and you are not allowed to be nostalgic unless you are writing a novel set in Cincinnati, because then you are being nostalgic for things that no one misses and that were pretty terrible in the first place and that you are now arguing in adulthood *weren't* pretty terrible in the first place. Because nostalgia in a novel set in Cincinnati is automatically cut with regret, self-hatred, sadness, irony, defiance—everything nostalgia (or anything else) needs in order to be worth anything. And if you are writing a novel set in Cincinnati, you are basically asking, If I'm not nostalgic for these worthless things, then who would be? If not me, then who?

This, by the way, should be the question every writer should ask him or herself: If not me, then who? If the answer is "Lots of people," then perhaps the writer should write something else. And this is this essay's final bit of inspirational wisdom: don't write like lots of people. One way not to write like lots of people is to set your novel in Cincinnati. Someday I'll actually do that, I hope. And I hope you do, too.

The Case for Meanness

One should always be kind ... in case it might be the last chance. One might be killed crossing the street, or even on the pavement, any time, you never know. So we should always be kind.

This quote is from Muriel Spark's 1970 novella *The Driver's Seat*. You should not pay any attention to Lise, the character in that book, when she says we should always be kind. She is psychotic, and also sad, and lonely. This—her sadness and loneliness—does not mean you should feel sorry for her. Muriel Spark, who made Lise psychotic, and sad, and lonely, certainly doesn't. Listen to the way Spark predicts Lise's future death: "She will be found tomorrow morning dead from multiple stab wounds, her wrists bound with a silk scarf and her ankles bound with a man's neck tie, in the grounds of an empty villa, in a park, in a park of the foreign city to which she is traveling on the flight now boarding at Gate 14."

Do you hear any sympathy, any empathy, any kindness, in that description? If you do, you have brought that shit with you. You

27

should get rid of that shit as soon as possible. Muriel Spark wants you to, or would if she were not dead, and so do I, and so does your fiction. That shit might be good for you, as a person, but it also might be bad for you as a writer.

What is good for you as a person is often bad for you as a writer. People will tell you that this not true, and some of the people who will tell you that are also writers, but they are bad writers, at least when they try to convince you, and themselves, that the most important thing for a fiction writer to have is compassion. Flannery O'Connor suggested in her essay "Some Aspects of the Grotesque in Southern Fiction" (1960) that compassion was perhaps the most overrated of all the fiction writer's supposed imperatives: "It's considered an absolute necessity these days for writers to have compassion. Compassion is a word that sounds good in anybody's mouth and which no book jacket can do without. It is a quality which no one can put his finger on in any exactly critical sense, so it is always safe for anybody to use." In other words, O'Connor suggests that compassion—as shown by a writer by way of her fiction—is important only to nitwits and cowards. Maybe some of you don't agree with O'Connor. The novelist, essayist, and John Calvin spokeswoman Marilynne Robinson doesn't agree with O'Connor. Robinson argued a few years ago in the *New York Times Magazine* that Flannery O'Connor was an example of a religious writer who failed to describe goodness. Robinson is right. This failure, and the pain, and the anxiety, and the art, produced by this failure, are just some of the reasons O'Connor is great. Though Robinson doesn't think so. Robinson says, again in the *Times Magazine*, "Her prose is beautiful, her imagination appalls me" ("The Revelations of Marilynne Robinson" October 1, 2014). Is Robinson saying that O'Connor writes beautifully even though she's an appalling person? After all, there are plenty of people who have claimed that O'Connor was an appalling person, and plenty of evidence—especially in her letters—to support those claims. But no, Robinson is saying that O'Connor writes beautifully even though her *imagination* is appalling. But how can we judge a writer's imagination except by way of her writing? If the writing is beautiful, how can the imagination be otherwise? What does Robinson really mean?

What Robinson means is that O'Connor's imagination includes an aesthetic (and maybe religious) appreciation of meanness, and this quality makes that imagination automatically appalling, and un-beautiful, to Robinson. To put it another way, Robinson believes that goodness is essential to a writer's vision, but as far as I'm concerned, goodness is responsible for Robinson's myopia. She claims in that same *Times Magazine* piece, "There is a lot of writing about religion with a cold eye, but virtually none with a loving heart." But when it comes to writing—religious or otherwise—what is so necessary about a loving heart? Especially if a loving heart makes you assume the absolute value of a loving heart despite so much evidence to the contrary.

In her essay "Imagination and Community" Robinson points out, "In the First Epistle of Peter we are told to honor everyone, and I have never been in a situation where I felt this instruction was inappropriate."

This is why goodness is no good for a fiction writer, or at least a fiction writer who believes in the sovereignty, the easy accessibility, of goodness: because she sees it everywhere. Because it is not dis-cerning. Fiction writing without discernment is still fiction writing, but it is mostly dull fiction writing. It is easy fiction writing. It makes things easy on the reader, and easy on the writer. There are no surprises in this kind of writing. All of Robinson's novels after her great first novel *Housekeeping* are sad examples of this, mostly because these novels—*Gilead, Home,* and *Lila*—are full of presumption: we all want to be good people, they suggest, or at least the best of us do. The books pretend to be folksy but in fact are infuriatingly condescending. They make me want to ask Robinson, and myself, all these rhetorical questions. Like, are we really to honor *all* our characters? In what way are we to honor them? If we honor some of them, say, by illuminating their dishonorable characteristics, do we not honor them? By writing mean characters, do we not honor them? By treating characters meanly, do we not honor them? Should we really treat all our characters the way we should, I guess, treat all people: with respect, with love? If fiction writing were a democratic process, a good-hearted process, then maybe we should. But it is not, and we should not, because when we do, we strip fiction of its ability to startle, to surprise. O'Connor knew this, which was why, in "Some Aspects of the Grotesque in Southern Fiction," she told this story: "I once received a letter from an old lady in California who informed me that when the tired reader comes home at night, he wishes to read something that will lift up his heart. And it seems her heart had not been lifted up by anything of mine she had read. I think that if her heart had been in the right place, it would have been lifted up."

Meanness is what makes that paragraph so great: O'Connor treats this old lady in exactly the way writers are not supposed to. Writers are supposed to treat old ladies with grace, and care, and compassion; O'Connor basically informs the old lady, with barely veiled contempt, that there's a big, beautiful, bizarre world out there, and it's a shame that she is too much of an idiot to see it, to learn from it.

But no, you think, that poor old lady. You think, she's probably very sweet. Probably she loves her sweet grandchildren. Yes, but those grandchildren probably know, when they're being honest with themselves, that their grandmother can be a real fucking idiot sometimes. That's why we need writers like O'Connor, who will be honest with their readers because readers cannot be as honest with themselves as they'd like, and with the eloquence that honesty deserves.

That thing I had the old lady's grandchildren say about the old lady was too mean, you might think. Probably. But I think sometimes that degree of meanness is necessary, and I think it's necessary because sometimes we get a glimpse of what writerly life would be without meanness. Take the great George Saunders. It is practically mandated that fiction writers love Saunders. I love Saunders, at least his fiction. I make that distinction because of his much ballyhooed graduation speech, "The Importance of Kindness," which exhorts the graduates of Syracuse University to be kind. The speech is fine. This is not an insult—graduation speeches are, at best, fine, and most of them are much worse than that. The speech is useful, however, because it illuminates the things that are so terrific in Saunders's fiction. For instance, in the speech he says that we eventually "come to love other people, and are thereby counter-instructed in our own centrality. We get our butts kicked by real life and people come to our defense, and help us, and we learn that we're not separate, and don't want to be. . . . Most people . . . become less selfish and more loving." All I can say to that is, thank God this is not true of Saunders's fiction. Thank God he does not use new-agey cum middle-management phrases like "counter-instructed in our own centrality" in his fiction (unless he's mocking those phrases, which he often does), and thank God most of his characters don't become less selfish and more loving. Sure, a few do, but in the case of those who don't, well, we're not meant to think kindly of them; on the contrary, we're invited to take pleasure in their misfortune, in their limitations.

Take the opening of "Sea Oak," from Saunders's second collection of fiction, *Pastoralia*, in which Min and Jade (the narrator's sister and cousin) are

> feeding their babies while watching *How My Child Died Violently*. . . . hosted by Matt Merton, a six-foot-five blond who's always giving the parents shoulder rubs and telling them they've been sainted by pain. . . . Then it's a commercial. Min and Jade put down the babies and light cigarettes and pace the room while studying aloud for their GEDs. It doesn't look good. Jade says "regicide" is a virus. Min locates Biafra one planet from Saturn. I offer to help and they start yelling at me for condescending.

Min and Jade shouldn't yell at the narrator. He's not condescending. He's a good, solid citizen, and it's important for him, and for the story, that he believes not only in his own goodness but also in the world's goodness.

But they might want to yell at Saunders. There is no generosity in his vision of their characters, unless we think of generosity not as charity but as clarity. And we should: what an act of generosity that is, giving readers the gift of seeing awfulness clearly! This clarity that would not happen if Saunders's depictions of Min and Jade weren't so honest, which is to say, weren't so mean. The world is stupid. "Sea Oak" doesn't pretend that it is not. It isn't interested in counter-instructing these stupid characters in that stupid world in their own centrality. On the contrary, it takes pleasure in revealing and crafting the world's particular stupidity. In other words, it takes pleasure in treating these mean characters meanly. And in doing so, takes the dumb meanness of, say, Matt Merton, and makes it art.

Of course, it's relatively safe to be mean to Matt Merton and his televised sideshow. The parents are on television, which means they're performers, which means they're shallow, which usually, in fiction, means that they're meant to be judged, meant to be damned.

Saunders's mean treatment of Min and Jade is riskier, and more satisfying. Let's see more of it:

My sister's baby is Troy. Jade's baby is Mac. They crawl off into the kitchen and Troy gets his finger caught in the heat vent. Min rushes over and starts pulling.

"Jesus freaking Christ!" screams Jade. "Watch it! Stop yanking on him and get the freaking Vaseline. You're going to give him a really long arm, man!"

Troy starts crying. Mac starts crying. I go over and free Troy no problem. Meanwhile Jade and Min get in a slap fight and nearly knock over the TV.

Notice here that Saunders does not invite us to be kind. Instead, we are asked to laugh at the narrator's stupid sister and cousin; indeed, we need to laugh at these rock-headed women so as to appreciate, and be part of, the world's mockery of them, so as to appreciate how much the odds are stacked against them, and so as to root, also, for the less rock-headed, more promising (though I'd also argue, less interesting) narrator. This story depends on meanness; it needs characters who exist to be mocked, dumped on, so as readers we can understand and be given a chance to align ourselves with those characters who are not. If we so choose. We might choose to align ourselves with Min and Jade. This is what makes a story great: it gives us choice; it surprises us. But it would not great if it asked us, and its characters, to be less selfish and more loving.

Marilynne Robinson certainly would not agree. Let's return, briefly, to "Imagination and Community" in which she writes, "The great truth that is too often forgotten is that it is in the nature of people to do good to one another."

Are you fucking kidding me? One only has to turn on the television (though one has the feeling that Robinson doesn't watch television, because everything on it is appalling, and Robinson might be right about that, which is why she'd be a more interesting writer if she watched it) to get an eyeful of people whose nature is to do bad to one another. But more to the point, can you hear the from-on-highness in Robinson's claim? "The great truth" according to whom? Well, to Robinson. But not to the writers I care about, and whom I think you should care about, too. Those writers believe that, as a writerly attribute or goal, goodness is not strictly wanted, because it makes you want to rise above. You should not want to rise above. Meanness—either an act of it, or an active cultivation and appreciation of it—requires that you sink in. That, as a writer, is what you should want.

Since we began with Muriel Spark, it's perhaps right to return to her—not to *The Driver's Seat*, which was called, in *The Guardian*, "a book of singular cruelty and misanthropy" (the reviewer believed this to be a bad thing), but to Spark's 1962 classic novel, *The Prime of Miss Jean Brodie*. Before I read this book, I'd heard it spoken of in ways that it made it seem like it was a Scottish *Dead Poets Society*, for girls. It is not. It is about a group of six girls in thrall to their electric, vain, hilarious, fascistic teacher, Miss Jean Brodie. But it's also an examination, and at times a celebration, of cruelty.

All of the girls (collectively known as a "set") are subject in one way or the other to Miss Jean Brodie's venomousness, but none of them more so than Mary Macgregor, "the last member of the set, whose fame rested on her being a silent lump, a nobody whom everybody could blame." In another kind of novel, this early description would set up Mary Macgregor as a heroine, a dumped-upon, geeky heroine with whom the reader is invited to identify and who, with the help of writer's good advocacy, will eventually rise above.

But it's clear from the outset of this remarkable novel that Spark is not interested in advocacy, or in rising above:

> "You did well," said Miss Brodie to the class ... "not to answer the question put to you. It is well, when in difficulties, to say never a word, neither black nor white. Speech is silver but silence is golden. Mary, are you listening? What was I saying?"
>
> Mary Macgregor, lumpy, with merely two eyes, a nose and a mouth like a snowman, who was later famous for being stupid and always to blame and who, at the age of twenty-three, lost her life in a hotel fire, ventured, "Golden."
>
> "What did I say was golden?"
>
> Mary cast her eye around her and up above. Sandy whispered, "The falling leaves."
>
> "The falling leaves," said Mary.

"Plainly," said Miss Brodie, "you were not listening to me. If only you small girls would listen to me I would make of you the crème de la crème."

There's meanness aplenty here. Certainly Sandy is mean to Mary, as is Miss Jean Brodie. The third-person narrator is mean, also, when she says that Mary is famous for her stupidity. Now, the reader might be tempted to think that being *famous* for stupidity is not the same as *being* stupid, except that everything in the passage suggests that Mary actually *is* stupid. But hey, she also dies tragically in a fire at a too-young age. And as we all know, to die tragically at a young age is to be sanctified. Is it not?

[Mary] died while on leave in Cumberland in a fire in the hotel. Back and forth along the corridors ran Mary Macgregor, through the thickening smoke. She ran one way; then, turning, the other way; and at either end the blast furnace of the fire met her. She heard no screams, for the roar of the fire drowned the screams; she gave no scream, for the smoke was choking her. She ran into somebody on her third turn, stumbled and died. But at the beginning of the nineteen-thirties, when Mary Macgregor was ten, there she was sitting blankly among Miss Brodie's pupils.

"Who has spilled ink on the floor—was it you, Mary?"

"I don't know, Miss Brodie."

"I daresay it was you. I've never come across such a clumsy girl. And if you can't take an interest in what I am saying, please try to look as if you did."

These were the days that Mary Macgregor, on looking back, found to be the happiest days of her life.

This is a wonderfully tricky passage. On the one hand, one might want to see Mary's death as tragic, and as the awful immolation of an innocent, a guileless woman-child who has been duped and betrayed and mistreated and who deserved better. But then the passage's last line makes that reading difficult: squinting, one could fool oneself into thinking that Mary is merely nostalgic; with both eyes open, one is more likely to see her as stupid. Or rather, one is more likely to see that the novel wants her to been seen as stupid. As this subsequent scene makes even clearer:

> Sandy, who had been reading *Kidnapped*, was having a conversation with the hero, Alan Breck, and was glad to be with Mary Macgregor because it was not necessary to
> "Mary, you may speak quietly to Sandy."
> "Sandy won't talk to me," said Mary, who later, in that hotel fire, ran hither and thither until she died.

The cruelty is stunning here. It is invigorating. It is invigorating in part because it belongs not only to the *characters* but to the third-person narrator (it is wrong, we learn as writers and readers, to conflate the third-person narrator with the author, but fuck it, I'm just going to say that it's the author's cruelty, too). The narrator is cruel because she gives us the cold, clinical, awful description of Mary Macgregor dying in the fire, and soon after we get the comic account of her running "hither and thither until she died." I say it's comic. I laughed at it, at least. You should feel free to laugh at it, too. It's there for us to laugh at. Because when we laugh at it, we become part of the problem, we are not exempt from it, and we are made to remember our own similar acts of cruelty. This becomes apparent in the scene that follows, during a class outing, when Sandy is tempted to be nice to Mary, knows that it would be right to be nice to Mary, is frightened by the possibility, rejects it:

> Sandy looked back at her companions, and understood them as a body with Miss Brodie for the head. . . . She was even more frightened then, by her temptation to be nice to Mary Macgregor, since by this action she would separate herself, and be lonely, and blameable in a more dreadful way than Mary who, although officially the faulty one, was at least inside Miss Brodie's category of heroines in the making. So, for good fellowship's sake, Sandy said to Mary, "I wouldn't be walking with *you* if Jenny was here." And Mary said, "I know." Then Sandy started to hate herself again and to nag on and on at Mary, with the feeling that if you did a thing a lot of times, you made it into a right thing. Mary started to cry, but quietly, so that Miss Brodie could not see.

In this scene, we see that Saunders is right when he says, in his graduation speech, that "kindness, it turns out, is *hard*." But the difference between his speech and Spark's novel is that the novel suggests that you can't do justice to the difficulty by helping, or allowing, or even wanting your characters to rise above the meanness of the world. It's no coincidence, either, that Sandy's dreaminess, her active imagination, her book-reading, marks her as the novel's writer figure (in fact, she later becomes a published author, and also a nun); on the contrary, Spark wants us to see that writerliness is not a failsafe against cruelty, but rather depends on it, which thus prevents Sandy from acting as though she's above the other cruel people in the book, and in the world. Which should illuminate something for us fiction writers: that the world, with its demands that in our fiction we be good, that we be nice, that we be kind, that we be compassionate, that we devote ourselves to the beauty of the *human heart*, makes it difficult for us to see that our job as fiction writers is, not to be mean for meanness' sake, but rather to find ways to be honest about how very difficult it is to be good.

What the Cold Can Teach Us

Here is something Joy Williams once said about Don DeLillo: "His work can be a little cold, perhaps. And what's wrong with that? The cold can teach us many things."

And here is something Flannery O'Connor once said about herself:

> Henry James said that Conrad in his fiction did things in the way that took the most doing. I think the writer of grotesque fiction does them in the way that takes the least, because in his work distances are so great. He's looking for one image that will connect or combine or embody two points: one is a point in the concrete and the other is a point not visible to the naked eye, but believed in by him firmly, just as real to him, really, as the one that everybody sees. It is not necessary to point out that the look of this fiction is going to be wild, that it is almost of necessity going to be violent and comic, because of the discrepancies that it seeks to combine.

Williams's new and collected stories, *The Visiting Privilege,* has been widely celebrated. No, that's not quite right. It's Williams herself that's been celebrated. *The Visiting Privilege* is merely the excuse for the celebration. That's great: both deserve it. But like most celebrations, this one is trying too hard. In trying too hard, it celebrates the wrong things. Williams has proven wonderfully immune to this—the celebration of wrong things in her work, and her life. In an interview with *The Paris Review* (the same one in which she praises DeLillo's coldness), the interviewer speaks about Williams's environmentalism, and points out that "Perhaps only Alice, in [Williams's 2000 novel] *The Quick and the Dead*, explicitly voices any of your political concerns." To which Williams responds, "Yes, but she's a crazy girl with a missing front tooth."

The celebration of Williams has focused on her God-hauntedness and her environmentalism. It tells us that her father was a minister, that she has lived in Laramie and Tucson and Key West and Maine, that she is fond of dogs and of long drives in old trucks. That she always wears dark glasses. It is curious: Williams may be God-haunted, but according to these celebrations, there's also something Godlike about her. As far as her celebrants are concerned, Williams is mysterious and contains multitudes; as far as they are concerned, she can do pretty much whatever she wants.

Williams cannot do pretty much whatever she wants, as she admits in her essay "Why I Write": "A writer starts out . . . wanting to be a transfiguring agent, and ends up usually just making contact, contact with other human beings." The way Williams can make that contact is through the crazy girl with a missing front tooth. That girl is the thing to which O'Connor refers, the image that connects or combines two distant points. The crazy girl is often treated coldly in

Williams's fiction. Meaning she is not celebrated. Rather, Williams is interested in seeing what the coldness does to her. Sometimes it causes her to grow in surprising ways. Just as often, it stunts her growth. Either way, the cold teaches us something.

The connecting image in Williams's stories is often a girl (many of the greatest stories in *The Visiting Privilege*—"Train" and "Winter Chemistry" from *Taking Care*; "Escapes" and "Rot" from *Escapes;* "The Girls," which is one of the newest, until-now uncollected stories—are about the relationships between girls and girls, women and women, women and girls). But sometimes, the image is a table lamp made out of deer legs. I'm speaking of "Congress," from *Honored Guest*, which is to my mind her greatest story and the one that distills all the qualities that make Williams a writer whose work will endure. Let me quote at length from the story's beginning:

> Miriam was living with a man named Jack Dewayne, who taught a course in forensic anthropology at the state university. ... [H]is students adored him. They called themselves Deweenies and wore skull-and-crossbones T-shirts to class. People were mad for Jack in this town. Once, in a grocery store, when Miriam stood gazing into a bin of limes, a woman came up to her and said, "Your Jack is a wonderful, wonderful man."
>
> "Oh, thanks," Miriam said.
>
> "My son Ricky disappeared four years ago and some skeletal remains were found at the beginning of this year. Scattered, broken, lots of bones missing, not much to go on, a real jumble ... your Jack told me they were [Ricky's bones], and with compassion he showed me how he reached that conclusion." The woman waited. In her cart was a big bag of birdseed and a bottle

of vodka. "If it weren't for Jack, my Ricky's body would probably be unnamed still," she said.

"Well, thank you very much," Miriam said.

There it is, all Williams's genius: the cheerful morbidity, the canned speech from a stranger in a public place ("with compassion he showed me how he reached that conclusion"), the odd-but-on-second-thought-perfectly-logical stunned response (because after all, what is she *supposed* to say?), the mordantly funny telling detail (the birdseed, the vodka). In this, as in most of Williams's stories, the protagonists seem to be asking themselves: Why I am so estranged from the world? Why don't I care more about it? Her characters are always waiting. They're waiting for something worth caring about to show up. They're waiting for O'Connor's grotesque image to appear. In "Congress," that image is a lamp made out of deer legs, a lamp Jack makes after one of his Deweenies introduces him to hunting. At first, Miriam resists the image ("The thought of a lamp made of animal legs in her life and *turned on* caused a violent feeling of panic within her"), but then quickly changes her mind: "Miriam could not resist the allure of the little lamp. She often found herself sitting beside it, staring at it, the harsh brown hairs, the dainty pasterns, the polished black hooves, all fastened together with a brass gimp band in a space the size of a dinner plate. It was anarchy, the little lamp, its legs snugly bunched. It was whirl, it was hole, it was the first far drums. She sometimes worried that she would start talking to it." Well, Miriam does more than just start talking to it: she falls in love with the lamp. As well she should. It is more interesting than Jack (who soon falls out of a deer stand and onto his arrow, which partially lobotomizes him, leaving him in the care not of Miriam, who is busy with the lamp, but the Deweenie who has taught him to hunt, Carl, who "smells ... of cold cream and celery" and who ends up loving moaning, drooling, half-paralyzed Jack the way Miriam loves the lamp). The lamp is the grotesque image that connects—the comic and the violent, the domestic and the wild, the light and the dark. Of course, neither Williams nor Miriam would put this in such a gauzy romanticized way: the lamp wouldn't let them. That's what it's there for. To present something worthy of romanticization that also makes romanticization impossible. "She looked at the lamp. The lamp looked back at her as though it had no idea who she was. Miriam knew that look. She'd always felt it was full of promise. Nothing could happen anywhere was the truth of it. And the lamp was burning with this. Burning!" This is the key to the terror and truthfulness at the heart of Williams's work: it is full of these grotesques; they seem, at first glance, impossible to love; she makes them worthy of love; but they are incapable of returning that love. No wonder that, in "Why I Write," Williams admits, "Nothing the writer can do is ever enough." Even the lamp made out of deer legs is not enough. It is both of those things—her ability to create the fantastic image of that has the potential to connect, and then her admission of the failure of that image—that makes Williams so great.

The Hate Mail I Got
When I Wrote about
My Hometown

I'm from Little Falls, New York, a tiny city (*The Only City in Herkimer County!* reads the t-shirt I'm wearing as I type these words) at the confluence of the Erie Canal and the Mohawk River, not far south of the Adirondack Park. Growing up, I thought Little Falls meant nothing to me, but once I started writing fiction seriously in my mid-twenties, I discovered that it meant everything to me. That I couldn't live without it. That I loved it. You'd think, then, I'd have no problem declaring my love for it in print, or in public. Except that whenever I talk about or write about upstate New York (I've written about not just Little Falls but also about Utica, about Rochester, about Watertown, about a fictional place called Broomeville that is in approximately the same place as, but shouldn't be confused with, Boonville—though whenever I write about the latter places, I'm really writing about, and thinking of, Little Falls, no matter the differences between them, and there are lots of differences), whenever I try to show my genuine love and affection for what I consider my home, I end up making a lot of people hate me. Take, for example, the response to an essay I wrote for the *New York Times* a couple of years ago. It's called "Do It for Utica!" and in it I facetiously suggest that the Danes move to upstate New York, or that upstate New Yorkers move to Denmark, as a way to solve our mutual underpopulation problems. I thought it was a fond, gentle satire, in which I show my affection for both places by poking fun at them, and at myself. But apparently I was wrong, at least according to this email:

> Greetings, You must realize sir that you cannot go about being an asshole all your life. I saw the article about Utica. May I ask, with all respect, who the fuck do you think you are? Have you even ever been here? Well, Let me state that after reading this my next communications are with the paper you wrote for, and it will be very specific on the issue of fuckheads like you sir allowed to have a computer to be an asshole. I was born and raised here, it is not the biggest or best city but-it also is nothing like the shit hole you live in inundated with fags, drug dealers, and hookers. Pollution and probably every non-caring ass wipe that lives in there! In closing-Go fuck your self! Allan

After getting several emails just like that one, you'd be leery of talking about how much you love a place, too.

Except that the email suggests exactly why I love the place, though there's sometimes a big difference between loving a place as a writer and loving it as a person. For instance, there are two ways in which I love Little Falls. One, I love it as someone who is connected to it. I grew up there, with my brothers, whom I love, and with my parents, whom I love and who still live there, in a pretty house with a beautiful view. I have friends there, and my parents have friends there, and they all mean a lot to me, and now that I have kids, we go back there to visit, and my kids love the people and the place, too. In other words, I love this place, as a person, for the reasons lots of people love lots of places: because it is full of good people, because it is beautiful, because it is interesting, full of hardships, but also full of hope and heart.

It is also not a boring place—in some ways, it is the most exhilarating place I've ever lived—but while my description of why I love it is sincere, it *is* boring. It's boring because it's generic. As far as my description would let you know, upstate New York is worth loving because of its smiling faces and beautiful places. Smiling faces, beautiful places, my friends, is also the slogan on the South Carolina state license plate. You know you're not doing your job as a writer when what you feel and write about a place would do well as a slogan on a state license plate.

As for Allan, my friend from Utica, his words would not do well as a slogan on a state license plate. That is why, as a writer, I love him. Or at least, find him useful. And for a fiction writer, or at least this one, utility is often synonymous with love.

His voice, for instance. All fiction—at least, all of my fiction—relies upon voice, a distinctive voice. Allan's is a distinctive voice, a voice that has range, a voice that wants to be formal (he begins his email with "Greetings," and he calls me "sir," both of which I appreciate), but also loves to be profane (he asks who the fuck I think I am, which is a fair question). This is a very literary voice and also a very regional voice (there are voices exactly like this in novels by Watertown's Frederick Exley, Gloversville's Richard Russo, and Albany's William Kennedy), a voice that really wants to sound high but is most impressive when it sounds low. A voice that is accidentally eloquent (which to me is the best kind of eloquence). In other words, a voice that struggles. The writer Donald Barthleme once said that he'd rather have a wreck than a ship that sails, because things attach themselves to wrecks. Allan's voice is a wreck; that is one of the reasons I'm so attached to it, and why I think there's so much for a writer to learn from it—namely, the literary virtues of anger, of self-deprecation, of being an outsider, of being from the provinces, and of being unreasonable (I especially love Allan's assumption that I am from New York City simply because the newspaper that published me is from New York City, when in fact the closest I've ever lived to New York City was when I lived in Little Falls. Allan's assumption is exactly one my characters would make, and maybe I would, too). These qualities don't necessarily make a reliable voice, but they do make an entertaining voice, a galvanizing voice, a voice you listen to, even when it is hateful. Because I don't want to underplay that hatefulness, especially the moment when Allan says where I live is a shithole inundated with fags. First, I want to point out again this combination of high and low (an inundated shithole is my kind of shithole). Second, this is what I mean when I say I love Allan as a writer: I would not want him to be in my family, or in my chamber of commerce, or in my White House (and this is why his hatefulness is significant to a writer: because when he uses the word *fag*, he's not so easy to laugh at anymore. Which then connects him to our larger hatefulness, and makes him bigger, more representative, more serious than most of us would want him to be), but I might want to read a book that has him it. Because who knows what he'd say next, and how he'd say it? Who knows how a writer might use him? Who knows how he might surprise us, and maybe even himself?

I'm not saying Allan's is the only kind of voice in upstate New York. I'm not saying it's representative of upstate New York voices. I'm not even saying his is the only kind of voice in my own books. But it's the one that speaks to me the most clearly, it's the one that inspires me, it's the one that helps me animate the otherwise generic ways I'd fall back on to express my debt to the place. You do not, as a writer, show your love for a place by making it generic, by making it just like every place, by making it seem like it's perfect, because when things are perfect they are boring, and then they're not worth loving, or hating.

The Facts about John Cheever

The publication of a great writer's collected works should be cause for celebration, or at least a measured reassessment. How disturbing, then, that the Library of America's release of two volumes of John Cheever's stories and novels was also cause for reluctant admiration, backhanded compliments, outright dismissal, petty personal attacks, and exclamations of surprise at how little this important writer matters anymore. As though the reporters reporting how little Cheever matters anymore have nothing at all to do with creating the sense that Cheever doesn't really matter anymore.

These reporters (who are sometimes reporters masquerading as book critics, and sometimes book critics masquerading as reporters) are wrong: Cheever does matter. He's one of the greatest twentieth-century American fiction writers, and one of the three (along with Flannery O'Connor and Donald Barthelme) most important American short story writers of the same period. This is a fact. It's a fact because I say it's a fact, and so you should accept it as such, in the same way you're supposed to accept it as a fact when biographer Blake Bailey claims in his *Cheever: A Life* that "Cheever is hardly taught in the classroom," and then when a "reporter" like Malcolm Jones in *Newsweek* quotes Bailey claiming it without apparently bothering to ask *anyone* if Bailey is right. Likewise, when Charles McGrath asserts in the *New York Times Magazine* that Cheever "is for the most part not on the syllabus," we're supposed to accept this rather than wonder, "Whose syllabi have you seen, exactly? Is Cheever *really* not taught in the classroom anymore?" Because he is, at least by me. That is also a fact, among other facts.

If it sounds as though I'm angry, it's because I am. Although not necessarily at Blake Bailey. True, many of the "reassessments" of Cheever following the release of Bailey's biography were really just slightly queasy, prurient plot summaries of it (I say many, not all, because Bret Anthony Johnston, Geoffrey Wolff, and the late John Updike all used its publication as an occasion to, if not praise the biography, then to celebrate Cheever's work and call for our return to it). And true, if Bailey hadn't written the biography, then perhaps some of those reevaluating Cheever would focus more on the fiction than on the life. But then again, Bailey edited both Library of America volumes, and it is impossible for me to be mad at him for that, just as it's impossible for me to be mad at him for writing *Cheever: A Life*, especially since I haven't read it and have no plans to read it.

Let me make this clear: Bailey had every right to publish the biography, just as Cheever's family had every right to approve of its publication, just as they had every right to publish Cheever's journals a decade or so earlier, just as Cheever's daughter Susan Cheever had every right to publish a memoir about her father a decade or so before that. And all of these people have every right to not give a damn what I have to say when it comes to their family, their lives, their stories. It sounds as though they've had difficult pasts, and they have the right to do anything they want with them, including profit from them financially. Just as I have every right to not read any of the above-mentioned volumes, while still maintaining the right to hold forth about Cheever's fiction, and how much it matters. And it does matter, much more than Bailey's biography: I can claim this with authority, even though I haven't, as I mentioned, actually read the book, and even though some of the reassessments of Cheever following the publication of *Cheever: A Life* make it seem otherwise. McGrath quotes Bailey in defense of his biography: "'The Joyce Carol Oates notion of 'pathography—the idea that one should not place an unseemly emphasis on the private of lives of biographical subjects'—that's nonsense, Bailey said, or a word to that effect." Well, it's not bullshit, which I assume is the word to that effect. A biography might be a necessary part of one's appreciation of a general or a queen or a labor organizer, whose claim to significance, whose *work*, is not already on the page. But a biography is not a necessary part of one's appreciation of a writer's work; in fact, a biography may actually hinder one's appreciation of a writer's work.

And this is why I refuse to read *Cheever: A Life*: because if some of the magazine and newspaper pieces on Cheever are any proof, then reading Bailey's biography immediately turns some readers of said biography into preening, judgmental, condescending *assholes* who, in not properly executing their reportorial *or* critical duties, reveal far more about their own limitations than they do about Cheever's.

Take, for example, the aforementioned *Newsweek* piece by Malcolm Jones, "John Cheever, Unappreciated, Gets a Boost" (February 27, 2009). Feel free to save your annoyance over the lame title, for there will be lameness aplenty ahead. Try to ignore the obvious schadenfreude when Jones predicts, "I doubt ... that the Library of America volumes will have anything like the impact of the publication of the collected stories, which ... sold more than 120,000 copies in hardcover"; try also not to wonder, rhetorically, if those 120,000 sold hardcovers—plus the thousands and thousands of copies sold in paperback—might not make readers thinks twice about buying another hardback full of stories they mostly already own. Restrain yourself from pointing out, after Jones asks, "Why should Cheever suffer eclipse while an author such as the late Richard Yates enjoys a renaissance?" that Richard Yates's "renaissance" can be attributed almost wholly to the fact that someone had just *made a movie starring famous actors and actresses* out of one of Yates's novels. Save your outrage for when Jones admits that, after reading *Cheever: A Life*, "mostly I just wished that Cheever hadn't been such an alcoholic bore." Such a careful, measured, critical response to a fellow human being's troubled life story deserves a response in kind: fuck you. Because in that one sentence, in which Jones attacks the subject of the biography rather than the biography itself; in which, rather than criticizing the biographer for either choosing such a boring subject or *making* him boring, Jones chooses to—viciously, snidely—wish that the subject of the biography (who did not *ask* to be the subject of this biography, by the way, no matter how many journal entries he wrote, no matter how many not-so-veiled hints he dropped that maybe, someday, he wouldn't mind if the journals were published) did not have a *terrible disease* that made him *boring*. And in choosing this, Jones has abdicated his responsibility as a writer, and therefore we're free to respond as he does, without decorum. So let me repeat:

fuck you. I seriously hope, Malcolm Jones, that Blake Bailey's next project is to write a biography of *your* life. I wonder if, at the end of reading that book, we'll find out *you're* a bore. I wonder if, at the end of reading that book, we'll wish you had drunk more, or that we had.

But this is not the worst of it. The worst of it is Jones's sense of fiction's relationship with the real world. The real world—as it pertains to Cheever, as far as Jones is concerned—is New York's Westchester County, where Cheever lived and where Jones lives. This latter fact—that Jones lives in Westchester County, the real one—is significant because it establishes Jones's bona fides: "When I tell people where I live, they often say, 'Oh, Cheever country.' I just nod, because the truth would take too long. The short version is no, I don't, because Cheever country doesn't exist any longer." Forget, for the moment, that Jones has already claimed that Cheever doesn't really matter anymore, even though he then admits that people immediately associate a *part of New York State* with him. Forget, for the moment, the nauseatingly world-weary tone of the local authority who has to *yet again* tell readers not to confuse fact with fiction, even though this local authority is supposed to be a book critic whose life is enriched by those who complicate the distinction between fact and fiction. What's especially infuriating and disheartening is Jones's subsequent claim: "For that matter, the world Cheever describes may never have existed quite as he wrote about it." He goes on to show how the men who populated Cheever's stories (wealthy commuters) were not really like Cheever (who was not wealthy or a commuter) at all. To this, the sensitive—perhaps oversensitive—reader is allowed to respond in this fashion: *What?* Is this not the point of fiction? Not to replicate the world, but to create a distorted version of the world by which readers can be entertained, provoked, transformed, educated in a way that cannot happen with the real world because they are too busy living in it? Is this not the fundamental purpose and premise of fiction, no matter what kind of fiction? It is tempting to blame Bailey's biography for all this, because clearly Jones has read Cheever's fiction as the biographical information has compelled him to, instead of reading the fiction as fiction. But no: it is not Bailey's fault when Jones complains that in his fiction Cheever "drags [his characters] through the mud because mud is all he knows." There is mud: Bailey's biography makes that clear; one knows that without having to read it. But it is Jones who sees the mud in Bailey's biography, in Cheever's life, and superimposes it on Cheever's fiction—where there is also mud, for sure, but, to overwork the metaphor, it exists primarily so that out of it something surprising and beautiful might grow. Jones, unforgivably, ignores this fact. Because it is a fact. It is a fact because I say it's one: because I've read the stories and not the biography, and I can see the proper function of mud in Cheever's fiction, and Jones has read the fiction and the biography and cannot, evidently. Later on, Jones tells us "Cheever is and is not a great writer." But given what comes before this (confusing) proclamation, it is impossible to trust Jones's literary judgment at all. The smart reader is tempted to run away screaming. And while the smart reader is running, the smart reader might be tempted to run—not to Bailey's biography, at least not at first, but back to Cheever, or to Cheever for the first time, to see what all the fuss is about. And the smart reader should give in to that temptation.

It is a thrill to reread Cheever's work—no less a thrill the twentieth time than the second. But how I envy the first-time reader of Cheever! Especially the first-time reader of Cheever who has some vague, dismissive sense of him as a bard of the suburban upper middle class, the quaint scribe for the postwar *New Yorker* set. What a treat to discover the formal variety of Cheever's fiction: the allegory, the fable, domestic realism, bildungsroman, metafiction, the ghost story, and best of all, the combination of some or all of these forms within the same story, the same novel. What an eye-opener when you come to his work expecting only Westchester County and also get New England, Italy, Egypt, and maximum security penitentiaries. What a feeling when you *do* get Westchester County and expect to find quaintness and instead find (in, say, "O Youth and Beauty!") a former high-school athlete and drunken hurler of furniture shot by his wife in midair. What a moment when you encounter the brutal, pitiless, matter-of-fact last lines of that story—"The pistol went off and Louise got him in midair. She shot him dead"—and then try to reconcile them with the mostly unironic celebration and lament of the life that led to the shooting just a half page earlier ("Oh, those suburban Sunday nights, those Sunday-night blues! Those departing weekend guests, those stale cocktails, those half-dead flowers, those trips to Harmon to catch the Century, those postmortems and pickup suppers!"). What a moment when you realize that this disorientation and these mixed feelings are precisely the point—not just of Cheever's fiction but perhaps of any fiction. What an epiphany when the reader realizes that there is no quaintness in the world of the story, that the only quaintness in the story is the quaintness you, the reader, brought with you, the quaintness the story kills off without killing off you, its carrier. What a feeling to have all your preconceptions proved so wrong!

What a disappointment, then, to not be able to write here about all the fiction—the best stories ("Goodbye, My Brother," "The Day the Pig Fell Into the Well," "The Jewels of the Cabots," "The Seaside

Houses," "The Housebreaker of Shady Hill," "The Country Husband," The Swimmer," "The Scarlet Moving Van"); the strangest, most beautiful novel (*Bullet Park*); the fondest, most loving novel (*The Wapshot Chronicle*). But there is too much great fiction, and one must focus on one thing in order to give one a chance to do all of it justice, and so I'll focus on "The Cure."

"The Cure" is the Cheever story that has meant the most to me a reader and a writer (to the point where I've echoed its ending in one of my own stories—by "echoed" I mean aped—just as I've echoed his use of exclamation points in this essay). Jones claims that Cheever "is and is not a great writer." I have no idea what he means by that. But this is what I mean when I say something is great: I mean, not that it's objectively great, but that I love it best. And "The Cure" is Cheever's greatest story. That is yet another fact.

"The Cure" is what one might call—with derision or pleasure, depending upon the "one"—a typical Cheever story. Its narrator is a white businessman; he lives in the suburbs and commutes (by train) into the city; he has marital problems; he drinks too much. Those are the details, not the facts—"details" being the things you need to mention and get out of the way before moving on to what really matters in the story, which begins like so: "This happened in the summer."

I've read "The Cure" dozens of times, and I confess I still get the chills from this simplest, most artful of sentences. The promise of doom in the "this," the knowledge that something has "happened" and yet we don't yet know what it is, the comfort of knowing that whatever "this" is, it will, in some fashion, be over by the end of the season. In other words, the first sentence makes promises so that the reader will read on to see if the rest of the story can deliver what's been promised. On to the rest of the first paragraph, then, in which we learn that the narrator's wife, Rachel, and their three children have left him, that this is not the first time they've left him, that the narrator assumes this separation is final, and that he's not entirely sorry about it: "She had left me twice before ... and I watched her go each time with a feeling that was far from happy, but also with that renewal of self-respect, of nerve, that seems to be the reward for accepting a painful truth." The narrator then tells us he's glad it's summer, because "it seemed to spare us both the immediate necessity of legalizing our separation. ... I guessed that she was content, as I was, to let things ride until September or October."

I love the false sense of contentedness here, the feeling of self-congratulation, the cheery notion that divorce, like medicine, might be distasteful but will eventually end up making you feel better. But I especially love how the attentive reader quickly grasps that while the narrator and Rachel might be content to "let things ride," Cheever is not. We know this because in the second paragraph there are already "a few minor symptoms of domestic disorder": namely, the cat and dog run away, and the maid gets drunk and tells the narrator that her husband has left her: "She wept. She got down on her knees. That scene, with the two of us alone in a house unnaturally empty of women and children on a summer evening, was grotesque, and it is this kind of grotesqueness, I know, that can destroy your resolution."

Here, then, is Jones's "mud": that Cheever won't allow his characters to get on with their lives, that he has to give them a hinted-at sullied history (that sly, marvelous "I know"), that he has to put this poor drunk maid in the narrator's path. The mistake, I think, is to regard this as mean-spiritedness (Jones claims that Cheever "begrudges his characters happiness out of stinginess or envy") rather than a dramatic device. Because what good is a story—as opposed to a life, I suppose—if you give your characters what they want, especially if they don't deserve it? Especially characters like the narrator, who manages to get the maid out of the house, and then gives us this piece of advice:

> You cure yourself of a romantic, carnal, and disastrous marriage, I decided, and like any addict in the throes of a cure, you must be exaggeratedly careful of every step you take. I decided not to answer the telephone, because I knew that Rachel might repent, and I knew, by then, the size and the nature of the things that could bring us together. If it rained for five days, if one of the children had a passing fever, if she got some sad news in a letter—anything like this might be enough to put her on the telephone, and I did not want to be tempted to resume a relationship that had been so miserable. The first months will be like a cure, I thought, and I scheduled my time with this in mind.

Another fact: this is a remarkable passage. Remarkable for the direct address, which the narrator uses to establish his authority and which quickly disappears, which lets readers know they are meant to resist self-help advice from someone who is trying so mightily, and still failing, to help himself; remarkable for the calmness of the voice, which just barely succeeds (for the time being) in keeping at bay the panic everywhere under the surface; remarkable for the portent of Rachel's phone call (Jones says that Cheever "was certainly no Chekhov," but here, in the phone call, is the Ma Bell version of Chekhov's gun that had better go off or else. Or else... what? Or else you'll be bludgeoned again with the truism about what Chekhov said about the gun); remarkable for the bald statement of purpose ("The first months will be like a cure"); and most remarkable for the way in which this narrator should be unlikable—for his know-it-allness, for the way he wants to put his family out of his mind and life, for that way he lies to himself—and yet he isn't. He isn't unlikable because, as Cheever suggests at the beginning at the story and then throughout, we lie to others and ourselves not because we are necessarily bad people, but because we want the lies to turn our life into the kind of life worth living. He isn't unlikable because we know that the missing dogs and cats, the drunken, jilted maid, are just the beginning of what Cheever will put his man through before the end of the story, when Rachel calls and the narrator answers the phone. He isn't unlikable because the world he lives in is so full of terrors and (compromised) rewards that the narrator is animated and transformed just by living in it. In the real world he'd be a sad sack; in the magical world of Cheever's fiction, he'll do anything not to be one.

I wouldn't use the adjective *magical* (so corny, so redolent of Disney and Doug Henning) if it weren't the best one available to describe the world of the "The Cure," especially if our definition of *magical* is capacious enough to allow it to include its opposite, or antidote. For example, as part of the narrator's attempt to keep busy and away from home and the telephone, he goes straight from work to the train station, and then straight from the train station to Orpheo's, "where there was usually someone there to talk to, and [where] I'd drink a couple of martinis and eat a steak," and then straight from there to the Stonybrook Drive-In Theatre, where the narrator "sit[s] through a double feature." I'm convinced these names, these places—the Orpheo, the Stonybrook Drive-In Theatre— were as magical seeming and sounding when Cheever wrote "The

Cure" as they are to us now. Because for us they function as a dream world, a hazy reminder of what we've lost and maybe never had in the first place, and for the narrator of "The Cure" they function in the very same way. The places are magical, but the people who inhabit them are human, the same way the gingerbread house was magical, but the children who entered it were not. The difference being the children were innocent, but the narrator of "The Cure" is not. All the better, as far as I'm concerned. Cheever's sad account of Orpheo's and the Stonybrook—the narrator says there's only "*usually* someone there to talk to" (emphasis added) at Orpheo's and he "sits through a double feature" but doesn't enjoy it—isn't a debunking of the suburbs (there is nothing as dull as a debunking) or of anything else, but rather a depiction of what happens when we bring our problems to the places we love that can't cure our problems and shouldn't be expected to. And when that happens, the only place we have left to go is home.

And home, in Cheever's stories, is where we have a hard time sleeping at night. Two things happen when Cheever's protagonists can't sleep: they listen to weather and modes of transportation (there is no better bard of insomnia and rain and train travel than Cheever, another fact this passage from "The Cure" makes evident: "It was after four then, and I lay in the dark, listening to the rain and to the morning trains coming through. They come from Buffalo and Chicago and the Far West, through Albany and down along the river in the early morning, and at one time or another I've traveled on most of them, and I lay in the dark thinking about the polar air in the Pullman cars and the smell of nightclothes and the taste of dining-car water and the way it feels to end a day in Cleveland or Chicago and begin another in New York") or they get up out of bed. The narrator of the "The Cure" gets out of bed, goes into the living room, picks up one of his wife's books (by Lin Yutang—and what a wry bit of scene and era setting this is! And how excellent that Cheever chooses not to celebrate or satirize the book, the era, the milieu, but instead understatedly reports, "The book seemed interesting" just as the "living room is comfortable"), and reads until, "I heard, very close to me, a footstep and a cough. . . . I felt my flesh get hard—you know that feeling—but I didn't look up . . . and yet, without lifting my eyes from the book, I knew not only that I was being watched but that I was being watched from the picture window at the end of the living room. . . . I looked up [and] saw him, all right, and I think he meant me to; he was grinning."

And then suddenly "The Cure" becomes a different kind of story, which is one of the things I most love about Cheever: how he will set you up for one kind of fiction ("This happened in the summer" is the way one might begin a ghost story), and then coerce you into thinking it's another kind of fiction altogether (the realistic tale of suburban sadness and ennui), only to then remind you that perhaps you've forgotten his original promise, but he hasn't, and he won't let you forget it, either ("you know the feeling"), nor will he allow his narrator to forget it. Though the narrator does try mightily to forget: he doesn't chase after the man at the window. Instead, he turns off the light until dawn, then goes to work, then goes to Orpheo's and the movies, after which he tries to sleep, and when he can't, he gets up and reads Lin Yutang. Notice the use of pattern and repetition (for Cheever, pattern and repetition are often synonymous with plot), and also pay close attention his use of talismans. Too many critics pay fetishistic attention to these objects, as though Cheever is using them the way, say, the television show *Mad Men* uses gray flannel suits and cocktails. Cheever's talismans aren't period costumes or identifiers; rather, they're dear objects that nonetheless fail to keep horror at bay, just as the Lin Yutang fails to keep the narrator of "The Cure" from looking up and seeing the Peeping Tom's face in the window. And what does he do? He yells, "Get the hell away from here!" ... "She's gone! Rachel's gone! There is nothing to see! Leave me alone!"

Yet another fact: it is impossible to keep one's spine from tingling during the reading of that passage. It tingles, not because Tom (as the narrator calls him) is so terrifying, but because the narrator goes from yelling the generic and expected, "Get the hell away from here!" to the unexpected and specific, "She's gone! Rachel's gone!" See: I felt the chill again, just typing those sentences. Because again Cheever has artfully mis- and then re-directed us: we pay attention to Tom when we should be paying attention to the narrator, to how he's trying to stop himself from feeling and thinking. This is testament, not to our limitations as readers, but to Cheever's expert sleight of hand. Once the narrator shouts out, "She's gone! Rachel's gone!" we are reminded, for good, of what's at stake in the story, to the point where the reader is tempted to wonder if Tom isn't the narrator's visible version of the Tell-Tale Heart: a manifestation of psychic terror rather than something objectively real.

He isn't; he is. The narrator discovers this a few mornings later at the train station: "Then I saw my man. It was simple as that. He was waiting on the platform for the eight-ten with the rest of us, but he wasn't any stranger. . . . It was Herbert Marston, who lives in the big yellow house on Blenhollow Road. If there had been any question in my mind, it would have been answered by the way he looked when he saw that I recognized him. He looked frightened and guilty. I started across the platform to speak to him . . . Then I stopped, because I saw he was not alone. He was with his wife and his daughter." This scene comes halfway through the story, and what a terrible moment for the narrator, and what a wonderful moment for the reader. Because we both realize the same thing: that there will be no easy answers or epiphanies or confrontations in the story. The narrator admits as much after he physically describes the family, who, despite their problems, are at least *together*, are at least *seemingly* happy: "I had wanted to know who Tom was, but now that I knew, I didn't feel any better. The graying man and the beautiful girl and the woman, standing together, made me feel worse."

This is a wonderful moment for the reader, not because the reader is sadistic, but because the reader is in the hands of a writer who denies the reader what the reader shouldn't want in the first place. If the reader wants the story to solve the mystery of Tom, then Cheever will solve it all right, but he denies the reader the easy pleasure usually involved in the solving of a mystery. Because once Herbert Marston is revealed, the more serious mystery remains: If the narrator's mess survives the unmasking of Tom, then how will the narrator survive the mess? It should be said that Cheever isn't any more sadistic in creating the mess than the reader is in enjoying it: because no matter what Jones says, Cheever is one our most empathetic writers. He doesn't mock the narrator's self-deception any more than he mocks the way the reader is so easily distracted by Tom. Because if the problem is severe enough, then of course we want to deceive ourselves; of course we allow ourselves to be distracted from it. But we should celebrate the writer who doesn't present us with easy victories, who empathizes with our wanting things we shouldn't want while still refusing to give them to us.

Should we have any doubt about him refusing us, Cheever dispels it soon after the scene at the train station, when the narrator goes to a party. What the narrator wants at the party is "a pretty girl in new shoes, but it looked as if all the pretty girls had stayed at the shore." Instead, the narrator gets a beautiful woman his own age, Grace Harris, who gives him a "sad, sad look," and says, "You poor boy ... I see a rope around your neck."

The reader won't be surprised, then, that when the narrator tries to fall asleep that night, he sees a hangman's noose, in addition to seeing Mr. Marston outside his window. He burns all the rope in the house, but that doesn't make the visions of it go away any more than the booze or the trains or the rain or the Lin Yutang has gotten rid of Mr. Marston. Things become so terrible for the narrator that he realizes "nothing now was going to save me," and the despair is so deeply felt and artfully rendered that the reader despairingly wonders, despite Cheever's light touch, if he really might allow something awful to happen to his narrator. In the end he doesn't, and how he doesn't is worth quoting in full before talking about why he doesn't:

> I took a train home, but I was too tired to go to Orpheo's and then sit through a movie. I drove from the station to the house and put the car in the garage. From there I heard the telephone ringing, and I waited in the garden until the ringing had stopped. As soon as I stepped into the living room, I noticed on the wall some dirty handprints that had been made by the children before they went away. They were near the baseboard and I had to get down on my knees to kiss them.
>
> Then I sat in the living room for a long time. I fell asleep, and when I woke it was late: all the other houses were dark. I turned

on a light. Peeping Tom would be putting on his slippers and his bathrobe . . . to begin his prowl through the backyards and gardens . . . I got down the Lin Yutang and began to read. I heard the Bartstows' dog barking. The telephone began to ring.

"Oh, my darling!" I shouted when I heard Rachel's voice. "Oh, my darling! Oh, my darling!" She was crying. She was at Seal Harbor. It had rained for a week, and Tobey had a temperature of a hundred and four. "I'll leave now," I said. "I'll drive all night. I'll be there tomorrow. I'll get there in the morning. Oh, my darling!"

That was all. It was all over. I packed a bag and turned off the icebox and drove all night. We've been happy ever since. So far as I know, Mr. Marston has never stood outside our house in the dark, though I've seen him often enough at the station platform and at the country club. His daughter Lydia is going to be married next month, and his sallow wife was recently cited by one of the national charities for her good works. Everyone here is well.

Well, we know, or suspect, that everyone there is not well, not really, which is one of the reasons this passage is so beautiful, so satisfying. It acts as a release valve for the story's terrible tension, while reminding the reader that the valve hasn't done anything to fix the source of the tension. Another way of putting it is that we know all is not well, but we also know that the narrator wants to believe it is. He wants to have hope, and after what he's been through, this hope isn't self-deception, except insofar as all hope requires a fair amount of self-deception. Cheever has done something remarkably generous here: he has made hope enormously difficult for his characters, not because he wants to drag them through the mud, but so that whatever hope remaining for them at the end of the story actually *means* something.

I've been talking mostly about readers so far, about what they might gain from reading and rereading Cheever's work, with or without the influence of Blake Bailey's biography. The same holds true of fiction writers. How much we have to learn from "The Cure"—about scene setting and genre bending, about voice, about pacing, about pattern and repetition, about empathy, about the inner lives of our characters, about how their milieu might gesture toward their inner lives without us wanting or allowing that milieu to stand for or be the entirety of those inner lives—and from the rest of Cheever's stories and novels. How much so many of us have already learned from reading and studying those stories and novels.

Except that Charles McGrath, in his March 1, 2009, *New York Times Magazine* piece "The First Suburbanite," says we have not: "The problem, perhaps, is that Cheever... doesn't lead anywhere... he's not an 'influence,' except possibly on a writer like Rick Moody." Unlike Jones, McGrath gets a good deal right about Cheever in his essay: He manages to keep what he learns in the biography from tarnishing what he sees and admires in Cheever's fiction; he pays attention to the actual stories and novels even as he pays attention to the life; he seems less willing to dismiss Cheever's importance simply by virtue of his recent sales record. So let's say, for the moment, that McGrath is right about Cheever's influence, too: let's say that Cheever hasn't influenced contemporary fiction writers the way, say, Faulkner, Hemingway, O'Connor, Fitzgerald, Saul Bellow, and others have. Might this be the fault of contemporary fiction writers, and not Cheever? Might we simply not be up to the standard that Cheever has set for us? Might we (so far) be incapable of doing what McGrath himself said that Cheever did in writing his first novel, *The Wapshot Chronicle*: "he succeeded only by reinventing the novel form for himself" (Oh, that "only"! If only more writers could accomplish something so "only" as reinventing the novel form!).

All that said, McGrath is not right: Cheever does lead to other writers. McGrath doesn't see them because he's not looking in the right places. When he identifies Rick Moody as the only carrier of the Cheever torch, he means, simply, that Moody has set much of his fiction in Cheeverland. But is setting the only gauge of literary influence and commonality? What about sensibility? What about Cheever's great contemporaries and near contemporaries—Bellow, O'Connor, Barthelme, Walker Percy, Grace Paley—whose work, like Cheever's, could be surprisingly experimental, or surprisingly traditional, depending upon the tastes and the expectations of the reader? What about Frederick Exley, whose boozy, articulate, self-wounded, self-deprecating, self-mythologizing alter ego in *A Fan's Notes* owes a great debt to so many of Cheever's conflicted men, from the tender yet rage-filled narrator of "Goodbye, My Brother" to the violent yet redemptive protagonist of *Falconer*? What about Russell Banks, whose now-you-see-him, now-you-don't first-person narrator in his novel *Affliction* is surely reminiscent of Cheever's first-person-narrator-as-product-of-authorial-will in "The Jewels of the Cabots"? What about Lorrie Moore, whose smart and smart-ass protagonists obviously resemble Cheever's as they both court and resist tragedy and disaster? What about Lee K. Abbott, one of our greatest contemporary short story writers, and, of the writers listed here, the one most mostly clearly influenced by Cheever, even though his work is set in New Mexico and Ohio instead of in

Westchester County? What about Padgett Powell, whose novels and stories, like Cheever's, push against and challenge certain traditional narrative forms without dismissing the forms and the traditions altogether? What about the new generation of fabulists—writers like Judy Budnitz, Aimee Bender, and Kelly Link—whose work, like Cheever's, treats sometimes-familiar settings in fantastical ways? Is this not an impressive enough group of writers for McGrath, or for anyone else? Who would not want to be included in such a list, as part of such a legacy? Who would not want to be considered a literary child of John Cheever? I would. And that is another fact, one that is probably obvious to whomever is reading this essay.

Of course, the risk (for me) here is that one could ask these writers if Cheever influenced them, and they might say, "No." But this is what happens when you love people: you see them everywhere. I see Cheever everywhere, which is why you should listen to me when I tell you to read his work, even though I've never lived in a Massachusetts coastal town. Even though I've never lived in the suburbs of New York, or the suburbs of anywhere. Even though I never met Cheever, nor have I met any of his family, though I spoke with Susan Cheever on the phone once, and she was unbelievably pleasant to me, especially given she had several reasons not to be. Even though I am heterosexual, not bisexual or homosexual. Even though I am not an alcoholic. Even though I have not read Blake Bailey's biography of Cheever, or Scott Donaldson's earlier biography. Even though I have not read Cheever's journals. Given all that, what can I possibly add to this discussion of John Cheever? *I have read his fiction. I love his fiction. If you read it, you will love it, too.* This is this essay's final fact, a "fact" being an opinion or hope that has the transformative force of love behind it.

Because all of this, of course, is the familiar cry of someone in love. When you are in love, you want people to know you're in love, because you want them to recognize the beauty of the beloved and ignore the things about the beloved that aren't so beautiful. Admittedly, you also want them to think, if this guy is in love with someone who is obviously so worthy of love, then maybe there's something worth loving in him as well. But mostly you want them to love the person or thing you love. Not because it reflects well upon you if they do, but because the beloved deserves to be loved. The beloved has earned it.

The Importance of Fiction
in the Age of Memoir

When I think about the recent popularity of memoir, I'm often reminded of a scene in Barry Hannah's "That's True," from his 1978
collection *Airships*. "That's True" tells the story of Lardner, a bogus
psychiatrist—he forges his credentials—but also a successful one
because he is "all fit out with thick glasses and a mustache and an ail-
ing gnarled hand.... He said people in therapy got close to a shrink
with an outstanding defect." Lardner tapes the sessions with his
patients, but "he never taped anybody without their knowledge of
it. All of them *liked* to be taped, Lardner said it was their creativity."

The problem in the story is not Lardner—though he is an unre-
pentant and unfeeling fraud—but his patients, who like their sessions to be taped. As Hannah makes clear, they like this because it
is easy to be taped, and it is easy because the patients' confessions
about their personal lives and problems is not a creative act but a
substitute for one. Hannah's criticism of this "creativity" intensifies

later in the story, when the narrator recounts one of the taped sessions.

Patient: I feel ugly all the time. I can't quit cigarettes. The two Great Danes I bought won't mate. I'm starting to cry over sentimental things, songs on the radio. Is it basically wrong for a man to like macramé? I never feel intimate with anybody until we talk about Nixon, how awful he was. My kid looks away when I give him an order. I mean a gentle order. Let me take a breath.
Lardner: Jesus Damn Christ! What an *interesting* case! Your story takes the ticket. This is beyond trouble, Mr. _____, this is *art*!
Patient: What? My story *art*?
Lardner: Yes. You *are* ugly. But so very important.

Again, though Hannah makes clear that Lardner is a liar, he is most critical of the patient, who is eager to believe that being taped is akin to creating something, and that the simple narration of one's life is art. Because if one's life is art, that means it is *important*.

I am not claiming that all memoirs can be considered the equivalent of Hannah's taped psychiatric sessions. I am saying, however, that there are certain cultural forces at work that make "That's True" more timely than we should be comfortable with. For instance, the most common complaint of the memoir is that it, like Hannah's psychiatric patient, has become self-indulgent, concerned less with the relationship between the self and the world and more with the self *as* the world. One only has to compare Catherine Texier's account of the breakup of her marriage—*Breakup*—and Mary McCarthy's account of her life in the 1930s—*Intellectual Memoirs*—to recognize the element of truth in that accusation. Both works are set in and around New York's literary world, but while McCarthy's memoir places an individual life within the context of a vital historical moment, Texier's suggests than an individual life *is* a vital historical moment. Tellingly, even Patricia Hampl, a passionate defender of the memoir, has admitted that "a lot of memoirs are self-absorbed, [and] many American memoirists in particular are screamers and whiners."

My contention is not that the memoir has a monopoly on griping, nor that griping can't be artful, but rather that we are in danger of mistaking griping *qua* griping for art. Of course, there are several reasons why we have put ourselves in this perilous position. For one, there is our growing sense that we simply have more to gripe about, more to reveal about ourselves, and that memoirs have become so popular because readers in the here and now need them so badly. Similarly, there is the sense that writers have finally torn away the veil of autobiographical fiction, and in doing so have given themselves and their readers an easier purchase on the truth. In liberating real lives from fiction, the theory goes, memoirists have liberated the truth as well. In fact, when novelist, critic, and biographer Jay Parini says in his essay "The Memoir Versus the Novel in a Time of Transition" that his students "definitely prefer memoirs to novels," he suggests that they are right in doing so: "I believe my students understand, intuitively, that when they read memoirs they are learning things that cannot as easily be acquired by reading fiction."

The "understanding" our students attain from the memoir—and the new wave of memoirs itself—has troubling implications for writers, teachers, and students alike. Creative writing teachers have long since, and frequently, experienced those students who defend their fiction on the grounds that it is based on truth, on something that "really happened." In other words, the work is in a sense already good because it is based on a true, significant event. This is precisely why we should be wary of the memoir: not because it is based on true events, but because it makes the aforementioned defense appear reasonable.

As we are fond of telling ourselves, we live in a democracy, where individual voices and lives matter: thus, the American memoir in particular revolves around the importance of individual lives. But once they are put down on paper, individual lives are *not* important unless writers make them important; individual tragedies are not meaningful unless writers make them meaningful. Critic Laurie Stone argues that "most memoirs fail as literature because their authors mistake their experience for a story rather than search out the story in their experience." And yet much of the talk around the preeminence of the memoir would have us believe that these experiences are important because they are true, because, returning to Parini, they enable us to learn "things that cannot as easily be acquired by reading fiction." But should our access to art be so easy? As Donald Barthelme once argued about his own fiction: "Art is not difficult because it wishes to be difficult, rather because it wishes to be art."

Barthelme's theory of difficulty is so instructive because it reminds us of what fiction can do to the world as we know it. Alice McDermott has suggested that fiction "tells us things and puts things together in ways that life doesn't allow, and by the way it puts things together, it show us things that life does not. So, unless the memoir is manipulating reality the way fiction does, memoir is limited to what life actually provides." In other words, if life is difficult, then we need to find ways to represent its difficulty; and we represent life's difficulty by adding to it, by putting it into a form shaped primarily by aesthetic sensibility, and not by our own experiences.

If many contemporary memoirs are indeed "limited," then perhaps we should reevaluate that most misunderstood of art forms, the autobiographical novel. Take, for example, Tess Slesinger's 1934 *The Unpossessed*. Slesinger was a radical writer and activist in New York during the early '30s, was married to writer Herbert Solow, and was friends with such prominent figures as Mary McCarthy, Lionel Trilling, and Max Eastman. Her association with these people ended disastrously as a result of various trying experiences: divorce, abortion, political alienation, physical dislocation. Given all this personal and ideological wreckage, it is surprising that Slesinger *did not* write a memoir. Instead, Slesinger wrote a highly stylized novel that combined and altered the identities of these historical figures, dramatized their failures and successes, and in turn reimagined the places where those failures and successes might take us. The act of fiction writing itself enabled Slesinger to illuminate her own history rather than wallow in it, for as McDermott says, in nonfiction "so many of the choices are made outside of the writing. But with fiction, all the choices must be made inside the writing." By making her choices "inside the writing," Slesinger made our understanding of a difficult history more difficult, and thus helped us see it in a way we otherwise couldn't have.

We should heed Slesinger's example precisely because so many contemporary memoirs legitimize qualities that we should abhor in art, privilege things that are "easily acquired" instead of things that are difficult. Not all memoirs are guilty of this, which is partly my point: we are celebrating the wrong memoirs for the wrong reasons. In doing so, we forget critic Kenneth Burke's still relevant admonishment: "art is not experience, but something added to experience. But by making art and experience synonymous, a critic provides an unanswerable reason why a man of spirit should renounce art forever." Writers, teachers, and students must reexamine what fiction can do and how it does it, in order to avoid some of the tremendous pitfalls that await us in the age of memoir. If we are approaching a time of transition, then our understanding of that difficult transition cannot be so easy as we would like it to be.

Why Good Literature Makes Us Bad People

We are living in the age of the Dumb and Destructive Rich White American Male Who Courts Crises, and so perhaps it's time to talk about his literary kissing cousin, that confounding strain in contemporary American fiction that I'll call the Smart but Self-Destructive White American Middle-Class Male in Crisis novel.

It's a sloppy term, an even sloppier acronym (SBSDWAMC-MICN), but then again, sloppiness is an essential part of the self-destruction that makes these books so wonderful, so terrifying, and so damn much fun to read even (especially) when they shouldn't be. And two of the most wonderful, most terrifying, most enduring of this kind of book are first novels: Frederick Exley's 1968 "fictional memoir" *A Fan's Notes*, and David Gates's 1991 novel *Jernigan*.

I should clarify at the outset that when I say that these books' first-person narrators are self-destructive, I don't mean simply that they are men behaving badly. Though they are that: both Frederick

Exley (the character and also the writer) and Peter Jernigan drink too much; they both have family problems (see drinking); they both have buddies (see drinking) who get them into trouble, and vice versa; they both are obsessed with their fathers, who inevitably have something to do with their bad behavior; they are obsessed with their penises, especially when they're not functioning properly (see drinking); they are both institutionalized, to no positive effect; and they are both dedicated to wrecking their lives and the lives of those around them. In fact, this is the only thing at which they succeed, their only fully realized talent.

But it's important to note that the narrators of *A Fan's Notes* and *Jernigan* are both *smart* and self-destructive; or better yet, that their intelligence is the fundamental part of their self-destruction; or better yet, that their literariness is a fundamental part of their intelligence, which a fundamental part of their self-destruction. These two novels are at war with themselves—that is, with books, with the things that books are supposed to give us and don't, and much of the considerable anger in these first novels comes from the realization that we're wrong for wanting books to do things—like *make us better*—in the first place. We can in part blame this want, this expectation, on the pressure our culture, and our universities, put on teachers and readers and writers of books, who, in seeking to justify their existence, constantly cite the practical, useful benefit of reading, as if reading will automatically make us better citizens. And we can blame this expectation on ourselves, too, for not being comfortable with the idea that reading books can sometimes make us worse, less productive citizens. *A Fan's Notes* and *Jernigan* are so important because they run counter to this prevailing opinion in our culture that reading books can make you better, or at the very least can make you *feel* better, like juice or medicine. Laura Miller wrote an essay in *The New York Times* called "The Great Books Workout," in which she asks, "How does one person's extensive reading benefit her fellow man? Or even herself?" Miller's answer is largely the same as Exley's and Gates's: it doesn't. Not only doesn't it benefit oneself or anyone else, extensive reading hurts, a great deal, which makes you wonder why we bother to read books that illustrate how bad books are for us, which is why, then, we should still read them. It is exactly this kind of elaborate hoo-ha, this kind of serpentine, self-referential, wearying logic that reading books can foist upon you, and we know this because Exley's and Gates's novels tell us so.

I'll start with the least interesting aspects of these two novels: their plots. Briefly, Peter Jernigan's wife dies in a drunk-driving accident (she was the one who was drunk, plus naked). A year later, Peter's son Danny, Danny's druggie girlfriend Clarissa, and Clarissa's mother Martha (who is also Peter's girlfriend), and Peter himself all move in together, and then Peter gets fired, and then bad things happen (drug overdose, suicide, gunplay, extreme emotional cruelty) that put the already bad things that have happened to shame. Exley's novel has even less a sense of cause and effect, or of plot. If we were to try to straighten out the timeline, it would read something like this: small-town upstate New York boy grows up in the shadow of his father, leaves his hometown to go to the University of Southern California, then travels to Manhattan, Chicago, Florida, Westchester Country, drifts in and out of insane asylums and alcohol abuse in a search for something—happiness? love? success? a comfortable sofa on which to lounge?—that he is never in danger of finding. But to attempt to straighten out this book is to ignore one of its main virtues. Early in *A Fan's Notes* (which is, in terms of real time, somewhere toward the chronological end), Exley crashes into a hotel room; in the other twin bed is B (who is pretty much a younger version of Exley) and a woman he's just picked up. The next morning they are gone, and Exley is left staring at "the untidy evidence of their urgency" on the sheets. This is a perfect way of thinking about form in these novels: both are the untidy evidence of their authors' urgency.

To return to these self-destructive narrators, what interests me is not that they screw up but the highly literary way they screw up—or rather, the way literature screws them up, facilitates their screwed-upness. These characters feel screwed up because they're so aware of the world and their distance from it, their alienation from it, and it's not simply that the books they read make them aware of their alienation, but that books *are* the things that alienate them, that make their lives impossible, even as they also make the mayhem so compelling.

One of the things that *A Fan's Notes* makes clear is that someone who *cares* about literature and language should never, ever teach high-school English. Early on in the book, Exley takes such a position at the Glacial Falls (NY) high school, twenty odd miles away from Watertown. To understate the matter, Exley is ill-suited for the job, in part because he assumes the vocation, the milieu, will provide a kind of haven for people like him, people to whom books matter. It doesn't. Books don't matter to the students, of course, as Exley shows in the following passage: "A freshman had nuns cloistered in a 'Beanery,' a sophomore thought the characters in *Julius Caesar* talked 'pretty damn uppity for a bunch of Wops,' a junior defined 'in mufti,' as the attire worn by 'some kind of sexual freak (like a certain ape who sits a few seats from me!),' and a senior considered 'Hamlet a fag if I ever saw one. I mean, yak, yak, yak, instead of sticking that Claude in the gizzard, that Claude who's doing all those smelly things to his Mom.'"

But Exley's main problem isn't with the students—from whom he is estranged anyway by virtue of age and education, if not by his own spectacularly juvenile behavior—it's with his colleagues, with whom he is supposed to have something in common, after all. And the thing that they're supposed to have in common, the thing that is supposed to bring them together—literature, and the love of it—is what alienates Exley so. Exley himself doesn't just "love" literature—love is too simple a word for it—literature is the only lens through which he can see life. The only vocabulary he has for articulating his needs, his fear, is the vocabulary of a reader. For instance, when he describes his infatuation with a woman from Chicago named Bunny Sue Allorgee, it's by way of Vladimir Nabokov's *Pale Fire:* "I had, like the mad Kinbote, lived my life in exile, waiting to sail back and recover my lost King of Zembla. That kingdom was always a 'dim iridescence'—a place above and beyond the next precipice; but I always knew that at any moment . . . the world's colors would fall into place and define themselves." Later in the book, Exley recalls reading Nabokov's *Lolita* while next door a married man and his mistress have sex: "I used to lie on the davenport trying to concentrate on Humbert Humbert's searing avowals of love while overhearing the joyous and erotic laughter from the adjoining suite, used to lie there dying of longing, envy, and boredom." *A Fan's Notes* is an extraordinarily lonely book, and this is one of its loneliest moments: because without literature (in this case, *Lolita*) Exley would not be Exley; but if Exley were not Exley (that is, if it weren't for *Lolita*) then he might be next door, with a woman, which one suspects would make him significantly happier than *Lolita* does.

It's not just that Exley's devotion to literature makes him lonely, but that it makes him a freak. Consider his account of Glacial Falls High's English department chairman, who "one day . . . told us he had come across the world *apostasy* but hadn't bothered to look it up as he had no fear of encountering it again." When the chairman asks his underlings whether any of them knows the meaning of the word, only Exley responds: "I don't know why I chose to speak. It would be the last time I ever did so at a meeting. I defined the word, trying to speak in a matter-of-fact, self-disparaging way, as though I were admitting that nobody but a fool or a freak would know the meaning of such an esoteric word." When he defines the word, Exley gets the expected response: "all heads cranked round to peer in utter astonishment and loathing at me, loathing not only for having com- mitted the gaffe of entering a discussion but for the suggestion that the world wasn't, after all, bordered by the town signs proclaiming Glacial Falls."

It should be said that *A Fan's Notes* and *Jernigan,* for the most part, resist the temptation to cast their protagonists as brilliant, book-learned, word-happy men underappreciated by the ignorant, illiterate world around them. Both novels are at odds with the world, but both also make clear that the world is *fine*, and that the novels' narrators are the ones with big problems. Indeed, the only way in which the *world* is to blame for Exley's misery in *A Fan's Notes* is that it lies to him about what literature can do, about why we read it and write it. Exley confesses that as an undergraduate English major at the University of Southern California, he has learned to believe that becoming a writer and a lover will help "allay the ache in [his] heart." Where has he learned this? From his professors, of course, and twenty years later, Exley laments that "none of my professors, talking about books in their even, slightly somber tones, had bothered to tell me that literature was born out of the very longing I was so seeking to repress." And yet, this realization doesn't make Exley feel any better—a bracing and necessary thought for readers and writers today, when literature is often advertised as an antidote for, and release from, longing and pain and loss. Indeed, when Exley passes by his idol, USC and later New York Giants wide receiver Frank Gifford, he wants to shout, "'Listen, you son of a bitch, life isn't all a goddamn football game! You won't always get the girl! Life is pain and rejection and loss!'" Life had taught Exley this, of course, and so has literature; but the key thing here is that this knowledge does him absolutely no good. Gifford is happy; Exley is not, and reading is a large part of what makes him unhappy, a large part of what has made him useless and helpless, and a large part of why he spends his time either lying on a davenport or sitting on a bar stool. Which begs the question: if literature makes you so miserable, then why would you want to read it? Exley admits that "I had incapacitated myself," but one suspects his reading has played an especially prominent role in this self-paralysis.

This is perhaps even truer with and in David Gates's *Jernigan*, though there are some notable differences between the two books. While Exley is often bombastic and self-dramatizing, Peter Jernigan is terse and self-deprecating; while Exley can be wounded and vulnerable, Jernigan is full of self-loathing, which in turns makes him lash out at the people he loves. Jernigan *wounds* as a way of not being *wounded*. And while Exley's main diversion from life's "pain and rejection and loss" is football, Jernigan's is television, which anesthetizes him in ways that his devoted alcohol consumption and Pamprin popping (as Jernigan himself would say, "whole other story") cannot.

These differences aside, *Jernigan*—like *A Fan's Notes*—remains important in our literature precisely because it shows the deleterious effects our literature can have on people who read it, and for whom reading means something. To say literature means something to Peter Jernigan is an enormous understatement. For instance, when his father, a painter, tries to remember whether the *Eclogues* or the *Georgics* is about farming, Jernigan says, "'Then you want the *Georgics*,'" and when his father expresses amazement that his son still remembers "'all this business,'" Jernigan replies, "You can take the boy out of the academy. . . ."

You can't take the boy out of the academy, it turns out, especially if he's introduced to the academy well before he's entered it. For instance, when Jernigan meets his college roommate, the first thing he notices is that the roommate looks like the literary critic Edmund Wilson (with whom Exley, by the way, is also obsessed). Years later, when Jernigan calls this (now ex) roommate, the ex-roommate asks him to "stand and give the password," and the password is from Beckett: "I can't go on, I'll go on." Jernigan even gets his pet names for his penis from W. H. Auden's *A Certain World*; he even, like an academic, *glosses* his own dialogue, as when he says to Martha about Martha, "'Beauty and utility we could have believed, but beauty and economy . . . ' Was this lighthearted or labored and obscure?" The point is not that *we* can't see Jernigan apart from what he's learned in the academy, but that he can't.

Does what he's learned in the academy make him happy? It does not, even though reading and the academy have, in a way, given him exactly the things they are supposed to give us. For instance, literature is supposed to make us wary—*petrified*—of cliché, and this supposedly makes us better, more authentic people because, somehow, if we are not using clichés then we are not using someone else's language. And if language is self—the theory goes—then when we use clichés we are not ourselves; more, we have no true self. But if one avoids cliché—and if literature doesn't teach us to believe in this, then certainly the *study* of literature does—then one miraculously becomes one's true, authentic self, not some tired, predictable borrowed self, and once one becomes oneself, one will be happy, or something that you can at least in good conscience mistake for happiness. Peter Jernigan has learned this lesson, clearly, but it hasn't brought him closer to finding some sort of true, authentic self; instead, the fear of cliché has convinced him that he is one, that there is no such thing as a true self, and the only thing that can even moderately protect you from cliché is to deflect it, inadequately, with irony.

For Jernigan, much of this has to do with life in the New Jersey suburbs. Here are his thoughts, for instance, on lawn maintenance: "I hefted the gasoline can: that plus what was already in the mower ought to be plenty. But if I went now and filled the can up again, I'd be all set the next time I had to cut the grass. Nothing like being all set." And after he's done mowing the lawn: "I put the lawnmower away and headed through the breezeway for the kitchen, forcing myself to stop once and smell the newly cut grass for a second through the screening. On the theory that it was the little moments that counted." Later in the novel, he takes the whole family to dinner: "Martha picked the Russian Tea Room and I said fine. I mean it could have been Mamma Leone's. (That was uncalled-for.)" What's interesting here is that while we take pleasure in Jernigan's mean-ness, Jernigan himself doesn't—in part because his fear of cliché has all but ruled out pleasure as an option for him. This is especially and painfully evident in his account of Judith, his dead wife, who once gave him a Powerful Pete, which is a "chrome-plated disk that goes on your key ring, with screwdriver tips at each of the four compass points and a cartoon strongman stamped in the center ... Its appeal for us was that here was this thing practically begging you to get a bang out of it yet you were too jaded to get a bang out of it. Which was in itself a species of bang. I don't know, maybe this isn't so re-markable. Big deal, we both had a powerful sense of camp." There is a real sadness in this passage—it is clear that Jernigan loved Judith, and he loved her for this gift, and yet he can't get any pleasure out of it beyond an appreciate of its triteness: his fear of taking pleasure in its intended purpose (in effect cliché) has made that pleasure impossible.

Though literature is supposed to excise our tendency toward cliché, it is also supposed to give us something in return (besides authenticity, that is): it is supposed to give us an inner life, which is precisely what nonbook readers (again, so the theory goes) do not have. Once more, Gates and Jernigan confound accepted theory. If reading has taught Jernigan anything, it's that he has not fully taken the inner life that literature has offered. The book begins, like *A Fan's Notes*, near the chronological end of the novel's events, with Jernigan in the trailer of his ex-roommate (the Edmund Wilson look-alike) in snow-buried, rural New Hampshire. Jernigan is there to commit suicide, more or less, but as he walks through the snow and the hemlocks, he thinks not of his wife or Danny or Martha or even his own death, but of *"the hemlocks and the peacocks*—or however the hell it went. That Wallace Stevens thing about the peacocks and the hemlocks. Then I tried to make up some joke, in my head, about the hemlock maneuver. And then the hemlock remover. A chainsaw: that would be the hemlock remover, although how would you set up the joke? Some inner life, boy." Jernigan's struggle to make a joke out of the poem, out of his awful situation, reveals that he *does* have an inner life, but his flip reaction to the Stevens poem suggests by comparison—to Jernigan at least—that he doesn't. This is true later on as well, when Jernigan loses his job, tries to make himself feel better by blaming the job for his numbness, and then admits, "Oh, completely my own fault: simply having a job needn't numb you. Obvious example: Wallace Stevens. Any deadass drudge can feel even worse about himself by thinking about Wallace Stevens." The example and the work of Stevens put Jernigan in a double bind: the poetry convinces him that his inner life is inferior, even though it's supposed to enhance his inner life; but conversely, he still *believes* in that the inner life, still believes in the life of the mind, except that the life of the mind literature has given him has trapped him in that mind. The novel is littered with Jernigan admitting that he "only lives in his own head" and that "I knew it was a bad idea to think about your mind too much." And yet he can't stop.

But why can't he stop? Why can't—to switch back to Exley—he be more like Frank Gifford (without disparaging the late Mr. Gifford's inner life, one can be pretty certain he wasn't burdened by the example of Wallace Stevens)? The answer is both easy, and awful: literature is the thing that keeps him a safe distance from the people he fears and dislikes, and for that matter from the people he loves. It's not simply that he's careful to note his fellow train commuters reading their newspapers while he reads Jane Austen and P. G.

Wodehouse; it's that Jernigan uses his reading—and the literary allusions he takes from that reading—to distance and protect himself from his son, and his lover. The academy often teaches us that reading opens us up to the world, but for Jernigan it closes off the world. For instance, when he quotes Hemingway to Martha—"Isn't it pretty to think so'"—she responds, "Why pretty?" and he thinks, "Oh well." Later on, when Martha confesses that she hasn't entirely divorced her husband ("I was afraid to tell you because then you wouldn't want to be my friend. Catch-22."), it's Joseph Heller who emerges: "'Something happened,' I said. Right over her head." The allusions are a kind of test: I dare you to understand me, they say, and when he's not understood, Jernigan seems to wonder: Why can't anyone understand me? Why won't I *let* anyone understand me? These allusions become just another addiction in the book, and like the other addictions, they grow beyond Jernigan's control: during a trip back to the site of his dead father's house (which has burned down, with his father in it), Jernigan makes yet another obscure reference, and then asks Danny if he understands it: "'I guess so,' Danny said. Doing his best to fake it. As old Dad was doing his best to shut him out by talking over his head. Christ." As this passage makes clear, Jernigan both loathes himself for these allusions, and yet he can't resist them either. Martha knows this, too: when she tells him, "And I can really do without the ironies … whatever they're supposed to mean." Jernigan replies, "*You* maybe." In a novel full of disturbing truths, this is among the most terrifying ones. It's no wonder that Jernigan—and one suspects Gates—views the following article in the Mind Health section of the *Times* with some skepticism: "*The creative muse is a surly mistress, demanding a hefty fee in anguish before she grants an artist's pleas for inspiration. Well, here's some good news:*

Alice M. Isen, Ph.D., Kimberly Daubman, and Gary Nowicki of the University of Maryland find that what creativity really requires is...feeling good." Jernigan "tries to understand why this was good news," while the rest of us wonder if creativity makes feeling good impossible—because while both *Jernigan* and *A Fan's Notes* are terrifically entertaining, insightful, compelling, *creative* novels, they don't make you feel good, they don't make you feel pleasure. Or rather, the only kind of pleasure they make you feel is the pleasure that is buried in regret: we regret that these lives and these men are so terrible, but we feel pleasure in the excellence of the accounts of their terrible lives, we feel pleasure in feeling the horror of them so deeply. Of course, that is not really pleasure, not as it's commonly defined, and if we are reading seriously (as opposed to productively), then we should not want to feel pleasure as it is commonly defined.

I, Grape

This happened at the dinner table, the site of many of my worst moments—most of them, these days, having to do with my younger son, who has especially rigid ideas about what he should and should not eat. On this particular night he had eaten a dozen grapes, and he wanted more of them. I, on the other hand, wanted him to eat a piece of chicken. There were plenty scattered around his high-chair tray. Any one of them would do.

"I grape," my younger son kept saying. "I *grape*."

"No," I said. I wasn't talking, now, about what he wanted to eat, but how he was making his request. You did not say "I grape," I explained, unless you were rewriting "I, Claudius," with a grape as a protagonist instead of the Roman emperor. If you wanted a grape, you said, "I want a grape." Lecture completed, I then waited for him to say, "I *want* a grape," so that I could then tell him that whether he *wanted* one or not, he wasn't *getting* one until he had at least one piece of chicken.

Instead, he gave me, then my wife, then his older brother that shifty-eyed, confused look common to young children and dogs. "I grape," he finally said, and didn't stop saying it until the end of this essay.

Rather than do something drastic, like kill him, I turned to my wife and asked her to tell me about her day. My wife and I are both writers and teachers. You'd think that this would mean we have a lot in common, and we do, but we sometimes have different ways of talking about that which we have in common. When I talk about teaching, for instance, I tend to use words like *teaching*. Whereas my wife, in talking about her teaching that day, referred to her "delivery system."

"Your *what*?" I said.

"You heard me," she said. I had. I also knew that that term—delivery system—was an accepted way of talking about teaching in my wife's field, and that, even if I didn't appreciate the terminology, there was no need to be a jerk about it.

"You mean your *teaching*," I said.

"No," my wife said. "I don't."

Now to be fair, to myself, my younger son was still chanting "I grape," and so the abuse of language as a subject was close at hand, and in my ear, and in my heart. *"Delivery system,"* I said, in italics.

My wife then said a bunch of things in reply, the gist of all of them being, "What is your problem?"

A good question, and I was afraid I knew the answer: for a while now I've wondered if reading so many books, and being a novelist and short story writer and a teacher, has made me miserable on the subject of the way language *should* work, as opposed to the way it often *does* work, to the point where I sometimes feel like Lewis "Teabag" Miner, the hero of Sam Lipsyte's great novel *Homeland*, who pines away for his ex-girlfriend Gwendolyn until he receives this message from her on his answering machine—"Oh, you must despise me. I despise me. But not like you must despise me. I've treated you so bad"—and who can't help but correct her grammar by shouting "'Badly!" at the answering machine.

I love this moment in this book, just as I love the moment in Muriel Spark's *The Prime of Miss Jean Brodie* when the characters debate why another character said "nesty" when she should have said "nasty"; just as I love Tobias Wolff's short story "Bullet in the Brain," in which Anders, a literary critic on the scene of a bank robbery, mocks the bank robbers for talking like stereotypical bank robbers. But it occurs to me that I might love these moments too much, especially since, in "Bullet in the Brain," Anders is shot in the head for his mockery. In Padgett Powell's terrific novel *Edisto,* Simons, the child-genius narrator, goes to another boy's house and sees this written on a handmade banner in the boy's room: My Goal In Life: Not To Be A Ignoramus That's My Moto. Simons remarks to the boy, "That's a good motto," and then to the reader: "I didn't know what to do about the spelling, so I didn't do anything." But how do you do, or not do, that? How do you not say anything when someone spells "Motto" "Moto"? Or even better, how do you say something in a way that doesn't make people want to shoot you in the head for saying it?

Meanwhile, back at the dinner table, my younger son was still chanting, "I grape," but he'd also picked up his fork by now, prompting my wife to end our argument and point out that our younger son had recently begun eating with a fork instead of his hands.

"Yeah," my older son said. "The fork is his favorite delivery system." If there was any mockery in his voice, it was gentle, fond; he'd said what he'd said in a way you couldn't get mad at him for saying it. My wife didn't. She laughed, and I laughed, too. *You did it!* I wanted to tell him, but he'd turned his attention to his brother. "I chicken," he was telling him.

"I chicken!" my younger son said back, the chunk of bird already speared and on the way to his mouth.

The Only Reason to Write a Novel: Paul Beatty's *Slumberland*

Early on in Paul Beatty's 2008 *Slumberland*, its narrator—an African American Los Angeles native named DJ Darky (who later in the novel becomes a jukebox sommelier in Berlin)—announces, "Blackness is passé and I for one couldn't be happier, because now I'm free to go to the tanning salon if I want to, and I want to."

This is, I suspect, a fairly accurate assessment of why Mr. Beatty writes the kinds of novels he writes: because he wants to. The great thing about *Slumberland* is that it does not ever give you—or at least, me—cause to think there's a better reason to write a novel than that the writer wants to—especially if it's a novel you can't imagine anyone else wanting to write.

Or if it's a novel you can imagine lots of people wanting to write, but in an entirely different, more explicable way. *Slumberland* primarily takes place in Berlin, during the Fall of the Wall. Lots of people have wanted to write that novel, and in fact have written that novel. But most of them would have, or have, used the Falling of the Wall as subject, whereas Beatty uses it as a backdrop for a search for a mysterious African American jazz musician who has written and performed the score for a piece of chicken pornography and who also may or might not be a Stasi agent.

Who would write about *that* when there's a perfectly good epoch-defining historical event to write about? Well, Paul Beatty would, which is one of the reasons we should be reading him now, and for the years to come. This is true of all his novels, including his most recent one, the Booker Prize–winning *The Sellout*, which is about another greater Los Angeleno, a horse-riding, African American pot farmer named Me who strives to segregate his town's school in order to put the town—literally and figuratively—back on the map, and who in doing so ends up being the reluctant master of one of the former child stars of the television show *The Little Rascals*. Meanwhile, on the subject of the deadly, destructive Los Angeles riots, there is only a brief mention, when a television reporter asks one of the rioters if the riots have changed anything, and the rioter responds, "Well, I'm on TV, ain't I, bitch?"

What is wrong about writing fiction about the Falling of the Wall? What is wrong with writing fiction about the LA Riots? Nothing, if that's what you want to do. But too often—and this is me speaking for myself and not for Beatty, though I really hope he'd agree with me—one has the sense that novelists write about large historical events not because they have something special to say about, or to do with, those events—not because they especially *want* to write about those events—but because those events are widely considered worth writing about, and because readers will widely consider them worth reading about. Which has the effect of making important events seem dutiful, uninteresting, which then has the effect of making them seem unimportant.

Beatty was once interviewed in *The Paris Review* by One World editor Chris Jackson, and when Jackson asked him, "Do you ever feel any pressure around your writing? For example, do you ever feel any sense that you need to have a more familiar structure to your novels?" Beatty gave this telling answer:

> "No, no, no. It's almost like how a Black sitcom will have a completely useless white character, or a white sitcom will have a completely useless Black character, to ground the audiences in something, to make sure that in that weird panorama, the viewer is like, Oh, here's where I fit in. I don't think I do that at all. I never even talk about it."

This is what's so compelling about Beatty's fiction: where other writers might try to figure out, to calculate, where the reader might fit in, Beatty is more interested in his own preoccupations—trusting that if they're compelling enough, trusting that if he makes them *seem* important, the reader will want to find a way to care about them.

Even if they're being asked, as in *Slumberland*, to care about Charles Stone, the Schwa, the obscure musician for whom DJ Darky kind of searches in Berlin. I say *kind of* because it's a thrillingly desultory search (and—spoiler alert—when DJ Darky does find the Schwa, it is thrillingly disappointing—sort of how it's disappointing when, at the conclusion of *Apocalypse Now*, we get to the end of the river and find fat, sweaty, mumbling Marlon Brando. Except that Francis Ford Coppola wants you to ignore the disappointment, whereas for Beatty it's the point). And when I say *thrillingly,* I mean that the search's desultoriness allows Beatty plenty of time to do what he really wants to do, which is hold forth: on Germany ("I'd soon come to learn that to a German, anything involving sexual perversion, punctuality, obsessive-compulsiveness, and oblique reference to the deep-rooted national malaise, was 'very German'") and race ("When I showed up to lease my first apartment, the landlord knocked seventy-five deutschmarks off the rent for reparations but wouldn't shake my hand to close the deal"); about music ("Wynton Marsalis reminds me that I was born wearing the wrong uniform"); on skinheads ("Thorsten Schick was the scariest person I'd ever met. An intelligent man who sees through the media thought control, the myths of race and class, and free market propaganda only to have become a guileless man who now hates without compunction and speaks perfect English . . . 'Just remember, DJ Darky, I don't have a beef with you, just your people'"); on empty American phrase-making ("America is always composing empty phrases like 'keeping it real,' 'intelligent design,' 'hip-hop generation,' and 'first responders' as a way to disguise the emptiness and the mundanity"); on the startling beauty of ordinary sounds, as heard by a professional listener and sampler ("That's a McDonald's straw being inserted into a vanilla shake . . . a video gamer vanquishing a turtle, capturing a star, and eating a large polka-dotted mushroom in world one, level three of Super Mario brothers"); on the special kind of loneliness a lonely person feels when far away from the people around whom someone normally feels lonely ("I was so lonely those early Berlin nights, I missed my own father calling me a dumb nigger. So lonely that I missed Black people, which is to say I missed people who can't take a joke, people to whom I was supposed to relate but couldn't, if that makes any sense"); and yes, eventually, on the Falling of the Wall ("I took out my minirecorder and taped the sounds of freedom. Cars horns blared. A woman slammed a pickaxe into the Wall, grew tired, and then began to spit at the bricks. Chanting. Clapping. People said 'Wunderbahr' whenever a reporter shoved a microphone in their faces. Cameras clicked. Singing. Flashbulbs popped. A beer-hammered young man, too inebriated to lift his head, vomited his first Big Mac onto his first pair of Air Jordans. His boys teased him about wasting a month's pay on sneakers that didn't even last him a day. All in all, freedom sounded a lot like a Kiss concert"). And this is yet another reason why we should read *Slumberland*: it believes that the best way for a novel to do justice to an epoch-defining event is to mostly ignore it for the majority of the novel, only to then compare it to a Kiss concert. Because unlike other novelists, who assume an epoch-defining event will be important to a novel because it was important to history, Beatty suggests that the novel has to make it important, and specifically, to make it important by comparing it to something absurd and self-deprecating and personal and trivial. In other words, Beatty suggests that what makes a novel great—or for that matter, what makes a novel a novel—is that it puts unlike things together, so that the reader will then wonder, Why would the writer want to do that? So that the writer can show the reader why. In *Slumberland*, Paul Beatty shows the reader why.

Artifice is Art: The Case
for Muriel Spark

The great Muriel Spark—who, over the course of five decades, published twenty-one novels and twenty other works of fiction, poetry, biography, and criticism—has much to teach us about the virtues of omniscient narration and the limitations of first-person narration; about the pleasures of meanness; about the difference in fiction between economy and minimalism; about the relationship between art and religious belief.... but in this essay I'd like to discuss what Spark can teach us about artifice and self-consciousness in fiction.

This subject has long bedeviled American fiction writers, who, on the subject of realism vs. metafiction, have acted less like writers open to nuance and difficulty and the possible influence of writers superficially unlike themselves, and more like participants in Battle of the Network Stars' tug-of-war (remember the William Gass–John Gardner 1970s point/counterpoint road show? A sample exchange from one of their public debates:

Gardner: "The difference is that my 707 will fly and his is too encrusted with gold to get off the ground."

Gass: "There is always that danger. But what I really want is to have it sit there solid as a rock and have everybody think it is flying."

But maybe, if we'd paid more attention to Spark's work—and in particular to her two early novels *The Comforters* (1957) and *Memento Mori* (1959)—then we wouldn't feel the need to continually rehash these old arguments ("Realism is the literature of exhaustion"; "No, metafiction is the literature of exhaustion"; or "You're not self-conscious enough"; "You're too self-conscious"), to take sides and then defend the side we've taken, defame the side we haven't. It's not that Spark makes a definitive case for one side or the other, but rather makes the whole argument seem silly. In these two sly, spectacular novels, Spark shows us what should have been obvious all along if we'd been paying attention: of course art is artificial, and of course writers must be self-conscious about it, but being self-conscious is not the end of a writer's responsibility toward her book (as one often feels is the case in, say, John Barth's fiction, or Raymond Federman's, or Ronald Sukenick's), her characters, her readers, but is simply the most efficient, most honest, most rewarding, most self-critical, most moving, most beautiful way of fulfilling that responsibility.

In *The Prime of Miss Jean Brodie*, the titular girls' school teacher is betrayed by one of her six favorite students (Brodie knows one of them is responsible, but not which one). Long after, she says to Sandy (who is, in fact, the betrayer): "You look as if you were thinking of something else, my dear. Well, as I say, that is the whole story."

[But] Sandy was thinking of something else. She was thinking that it was not the whole story." This is an excellent way of describing self-consciousness and artifice in Spark's work: it is part of the story, but it is not the whole story.

To begin at the beginning (which is where neither of these two novels begin): Spark's first novel, *The Comforters*. It's a novel about jewels being smuggled in loaves of bread and tins of fish by aging and crippled smugglers, and it's also a novel about diabolism, bigamy, Catholicism, and homosexuality. It features a character who, when not in contact with other characters, disappears entirely from the book because she has no private life, and it features another character (Caroline, one of the two protagonists) who hears the novel itself being typed and narrated. At the book's opening we find Laurence (the other main character and Caroline's on and off boyfriend) at his grandmother's house, snooping around her bedroom dresser:

> He counted three hairpins, eight mothballs; he found a small piece of black velvet embroidered with jet beads now loose on their thread. He reckoned the bit of stuff would be about 2 1/2 inches by 1 1/2. In another drawer he found a comb with some of his grandmother's hair on it and noted that the object was none too neat. He got some pleasure from having met with these facts, three hairpins, eight mothballs, a comb none too neat, the property of his grandmother, here in her home in Sussex, now in the present tense. That is what Laurence was like.
>
> "It is unhealthy," his mother had lately told him. "It's the only unhealthy thing about your mind, the way you notice absurd details, it's absurd of you."
>
> "That's what I'm like," Laurence said.

Like Laurence, the reader gets "some pleasure from having met with these facts." But I'd especially like to call attention to the way the phrase "That is what Laurence was like," appears first in narration, and then, slightly modified, in Laurence's dialogue. In other words, Spark puts words into her character's mouth, and we know Spark puts words into her character's mouth because she lets us read the words in the omniscient narration before she puts them there.

Putting words into your characters' mouths is, of course, exactly what writers are repeatedly told they shouldn't do, which long ago should have forced us to ask: Well, who else is going to put them there? Ernest Hemingway, the Great Bwana of realism, famously advised writers, "Write the truest sentence you know." As far as pieces of writerly advice go, this isn't particularly useful (I imagine someone diligently making a to-do list of this stuff, hoping someday to be able to cross it off the list: Write the truest sentence you know? Check), and so to help us out, Hemingway gives us a counterexample in his story "Nobody Ever Dies," in which one character tells another, "You talk like a book." The story leaves us no doubt that this is supposed to be a bad thing. The worst thing. The least true thing.

If it is frowned upon, in a realistic novel, to have your characters talk like a book, then no wonder Spark has Caroline—who, like nearly all of Spark's main characters, is a stand in for Spark herself, and who is also a literary critic writing a book called *Form in the Modern Novel*—admit, "I'm having difficulty with the chapter on realism"? Caroline's problem with realism is also Spark's problem, and it's clear that she's both confrontational and defensive when Caroline tells her priest about how she can hear the novel being narrated to her: "'But the typewriter and the voices—it is as if a writer on another plane of existence was writing a story about us.' As soon as she had said these words, Caroline knew that she had hit on the truth. After that she said no more to him on the subject."

Caroline doesn't have to say anything more, because Spark makes sure the reader knows that *she* is the person writing the novel, that she is not only writing the dialogue, but feeding her characters their lines. And one of the ways she makes sure we know this is by having omniscient narrative directly infect, or influence (depending on your feeling about such a relationship), the characters' dialogue, as in this passage, when the narrator says about Caroline, "That did amuse her," and then Caroline immediately says to Laurence, "That does amuse me." Likewise, we learn that "even as he spoke Laurence knew that phrases like 'your very own' and 'dear little house' betrayed what he was leading up to, they were not his grandmother's style," and then his grandmother immediately says, "I know what you're leading up to." It's as though the characters have access to each others' thoughts, which of course they do, since Spark gave them the thoughts, put them in their heads, just as she put the words in their mouths to respond to (and mimic) the thoughts. She has done exactly what so many people have said writers should not do: she has her characters talk (and think) like a book, specifically a Muriel Spark book.

I mention this because I know of no other writer who so boldly flouts this conventional wisdom, who draws so much attention to the artifice of her characters' dialogue, who so insistently makes plain that she's the source of it, and who has no desire to pretend that her characters talk "naturally." But why? It would be one thing if Spark were motivated by mere cleverness (as seems to be true of so many of the lesser metafictionists of the 1970s). But Spark has something else on her mind, and the key to it is the way her characters speak. When people demand that characters speak "naturally," I take "naturally" to mean "purely"—that is, not influenced or infected by their creator. But as Spark shows, this theory needlessly hamstrings the writer, and alienates her characters. Yes, Spark self-consciously puts words in her characters' mouths. Yes, she lets us know that she has characters mimic each other, which is to say, mimic the thoughts Spark has put in their heads, mimic the words she's put in their mouths. But as Spark makes clear, mimicry isn't an impediment to the truest thing, but the most direct path to it. Mimicry isn't natural dialogue, but rather, in Spark's hands, something superior to it. If natural dialogue distinguishes characters from one another, then mimicry shows how close they are to each other, how well they know each other. It brings them closer together.

Take, for instance, *Memento Mori*. In this novel a group of old friends (that is, a group of old people who have known each other and been friends, enemies, lovers, ex-lovers, etc., for a very long time) keep receiving anonymous phone calls in which the caller says, "Remember you must die," and then hangs up. The novel is a meditation on mortality, of course, but it's also a meditation on how the people we love and hate influence the way we think and speak. For instance, when Dame Lettie accuses Miss Taylor of speaking like another character, Miss Taylor says, "I must . . . have caught a lot of her ways of thought and speech." As Spark makes clear, this is a necessary, wanted virus. The common charge against artificial dialogue is that it limits our sense of the characters, and makes the characters themselves predictable. When writers put words in their characters' mouths, this theory goes, the characters become flat. Or, as many of her critics have complained, when Spark puts words in her characters' mouths, she, and her books, seem removed from, and condescending toward, their problems. But a careful reading of Spark's early work suggests otherwise: the more limited and artificial the characters' dialogue, the better they know each other, the closer they are to each other, and thus they closer we are to them. Dame Lettie and Miss Taylor reveal this in the following passage: "Dame Lettie thought, She is jealous of anyone else's having to do with Charmain [another character being told to remember she must die]. Perhaps I am, thought Miss Taylor who could read Dame Lettie's idea." These characters know each other—and we know them—so well, not because they talk naturally, but because they talk like their author makes them talk, and because their author makes sure we know it.

This may sound limited and knowing, but it's not, in part because Spark uses this sense of artifice as a way to enhance, and gesture toward, a sense of mystery in each of her novels. In doing so, she also gives us another, better answer to the tired question, "Do your characters ever surprise you?" On the one hand is Nabokov's infamous line in which he compares his characters to galley slaves who do what he wants them to do. On the other hand is the more common, and more fatuous, writerly claim that one's characters have minds of their own and the writer is simply obeying their commands (which makes it easy for said writer to avoid taking responsibility for writing a terrible book).

Like Nabokov, Spark makes it clear that her characters do, or at least say, what she wants them to. And in doing so, she also admits to being aware of her characters', and her books', possible limitations, as in *The Comforters* when Caroline tells a friend, "'The Typing Ghost has not recorded any lively details about this hospital ward. The reason is that the author doesn't know how to describe a hospital ward.

This interlude in my life is not part of the book in consequence.' It was by making exasperating remarks like this that Caroline Rose continued to interfere with the book."

This a terrific, bracing moment, one that says much about Spark, and what we can learn from her. For instance, it teaches us that if you are going to write a novel about the writing of a novel—and more generally, if you're going to write a novel that's self-conscious about itself, a novel that trumpets its sense of artifice—then you'd better be self-deprecating about it (something that many of the aforementioned lesser metafictionists—lesser because they seem so self-pleased with their self-consciousness—never seemed to have realized). For another, it teaches us that in writing such a self-conscious book, one must constantly make sure the novel is leading us toward something beyond its own artifice. The conflict between Caroline and the Typing Ghost (or Spark) is really a dramatization of the novel's, any great novel's, main question, which is: what is going to happen? What is the significance of the mystery? Will it be solved? In the case of *The Comforters*, will we—and Caroline—find out who is really writing the novel, or if anyone is? In the case of *Memento Mori*, will we—and all the ancient characters that are to remember they must die—find out who is making these mysterious phone calls? And if not, what is going to happen to these characters whom we know so well, and who know each other so well, because of, and not despite, the words being put into their mouths? If the seemingly omnipotent author, who has made these characters (as she frequently lets us know), isn't capable of solving the mystery, then who is?

Toward the end of *Memento Mori*, Mortimer, the detective investigating the mysterious phone calls, gets one himself: "Within a few seconds, he put down the receiver. How strange, he thought, that mine is always a woman. Everyone else gets a man on the line to them, but mine is always this woman, gentle-spoken and respectful." And at the very end of *The Comforters*, Laurence is infuriated by Caroline writing a novel, pens her a letter listing his objections, then tears up the letter: "He saw the bits of paper come to rest, some on the scrubby ground, some among the deep marsh weeds, and one piece on a thorn-bush; and he did not foresee his later wonder, with a curious rejoicing, how the letter had got into the book." It is remarkable that two novels so ruthlessly manipulated by their author, so full of artifice, could produce such a sense of genuine wonder, of genuine surprise. But we would not find the sense of wonder and surprise so genuine if the artifice weren't so expertly, and purposefully, executed. And fiction writers and readers would not be able to so completely buy into the supposed divisions in contemporary American fiction between realism and metafiction, between mimesis and self-consciousness, if we read the late, great Muriel Spark as she deserves to be read: with our minds and eyes open to the possibility that we have something to learn from artful artifice, with our hearts open to the sense of wonder when we do.

The Problem of Place

Writers are told (often dumbly, automatically) to write about what we know. And one of the things we know, or think we know, is the place we grew up. It's no surprise, then, that place has become a fetish for fiction writers. Take, for instance, Lee Smith's claim that "a writer can't choose her material. You are given it. It's where you grow up." Similarly, Tim Gautreaux posits that one's fictional world is most profitably the "territory he was born into." Moreover, Gautreaux says that he "can't understand these people who say that they can write about anything and any time if they do enough research, because when they say that, they cut themselves off from the speech of those they grew up with. . . . Sometimes [Gautreaux admits] I try to set a story in another region of the country, and it's harder for me to write those stories."

But should fiction ever be easy? Should it ever be comfortable? Gautreaux's and Smith's comments suggest why place has become a limiting mechanism in fiction—not because place intrinsically binds or constricts a writer's imagination, but because too many writers *value* its ability to bind or constrict. Too often, the urge to "stay put" has made contemporary fiction terribly safe, both stylistically and intellectually.

How then to place "place" as a fiction writer, and a teacher of fiction writing? One thing *not* to do is to insist that a strong attachment to place in fiction is bankrupt; instead, it's better to insist that writers be hyperconscious of the potentially clichéd ground on which they plan to trod. One of the best models of this kind of hyperconscious treatment of place is the aforementioned Padgett Powell, who grounds his fiction in the South (Florida and South Carolina mostly) so that he might disturb the ground itself, and not allow himself (and his reader) to take root in it. For instance, at the beginning of his story "Trick or Treat," from his collection *Aliens of Affection*, the protagonist, Mrs. Hollingsworth, walks to the grocery store while saying, "It loves me, it loves me not. I love *it*, I love *it* not." When a boy asks her to what she's referring, she says, "The South." "What's that?" the boy asks. Her response:

> "This," Mrs. Hollingsworth said, indicating with her arm the trees and air and houses and suspiring history and ennui and corruption and meanness and game violators and bottomland and chivalric humanism and people who are smart about money and people who don't have a clue and heroism and stray pets around them.

The boy asks her if she's lost her mind. Well, she has and she hasn't; but the boy wouldn't have asked the question if Mrs. Hollingsworth were a recognizable southern character—that is, if she were one of the Memaws and Pawpaws that dominate the least interesting kind of southern fiction. But she's not, and the boy can't get a fix on her, and thus she is dangerous, productively so. In this way, Powell shows us that fiction can and should call into the question the sanctity of place, to satirize the sentimental conventions—literary and otherwise—associated with place, to make it more dangerous, more knowing, more intelligent even through its evocation of cluelessness.

It is maybe obvious that several of the writers mentioned thus far are from the South, were born in the South or lived in the South or were related to someone who lived in the South or set their work in the South. This is no accident: southern literature is the most prominent form of regional literature in our country (before any of us get our knickers in a twist over this, let me say that I think it's a possible sign of a region's healthy literary culture that it doesn't have a prominent and easily definable regional literature)., Whether this is because southern writers have a stronger sense of their region than those from other regions, or whether it's because southern writers are natural-born storytellers, or whether it's because there is such a strong literary tradition in the South to defend, to honor, to continue, to fight with, to live down, I'm loath to say. Clearly, though, it is difficult to talk about place in contemporary fiction without talking about southern fiction, which is why I would dearly love not to talk about it here. The problem with the discussion—the discussion I don't want to have—is not that it isn't potentially interesting (as Powell says in his essay "What Southern Literature Is": "The question What is Southern Literature?, were it not asked perpetually by so many persons presumably not uninterested in knowing the answer, would seem to be a question profoundly uninteresting"), but rather that so many people asking the question aren't interested in the question itself, but in showing that they know the answer. This is the same problem in the approach many writers take in regard to place in their fiction: they set a story in a particular place, not because of the place's mystery, but because they know it so well. Or they think they know it so well.

This came up in one of my fiction workshops at Bowdoin (which is in Brunswick, Maine). Right before class, as we were talking about the weather, how odd and end-of-days-ish it had been, one poor student, a Maine native and expert on all things northern New England, said, "Well, as we say in Maine, if you don't like the weather, then just wait a minute." I laughed and told him that in every place I had ever lived (New York, Ohio, Pennsylvania, South Carolina, Massachusetts, even southern California) people had said the exact same thing about their state's weather, and that when it came to homespun aphorisms regarding the meteorological, the citizens of Maine were absolutely no different than the citizens of Ohio. The student just looked at me as if I'd told him that his mother was not actually his mother. By the end of class he still hadn't gotten over it. There's a chance he may never get over it.

But back to place and contemporary fiction: one could do the easy thing and suggest that writers set stories in a less familiar place, a place they don't know so well, or a place that has been written about infrequently, a place about which readers and writers both will have fewer preconceived notions. Of course, you can't and shouldn't tell people not to set a story in one place or to set it in another, but it is true that some places are less fraught, in literary terms, than others. Much of my own fiction is set in upstate New York, for instance, and one of the great advantages to setting a story in upstate New York (though this is not the reason my work is set there) is that you have so little to live down, and so diffuse a literary tradition with which to compete. After all, what is the upstate New York literary tradition? Of all the great novelists who have set their work there—James Fenimore Cooper, Joyce Carol Oates, Theodore Dreiser, Russell Banks, William Kennedy, Richard Russo—can they really be said to be upstate New York writers, or to have a formed a canon of upstate New York fiction? And perhaps more to the point for our students, do most readers already have a firm idea of what authentic upstate New Yorkers sound like?

But still, the problem remains: yes, there *are* a few people out there who already have a firm idea of what an authentic upstate New Yorker—or an authentic New Mexican, or an authentic South Side Chicagoan—sounds like. And no matter what the premise or form or tone of your work, no matter how outrageous or incongruous your characters, no matter if you've written a cornpone *Coriolanus* or a Demeter in Albuquerque, there will be a reader of the work who will say, "I'm from Albuquerque, and people there really don't talk like that." As troubling, if such a story comes under fire in the workshop for its implausibility, is when the writer then defends his work in much the same way. In other words, if one's work is set in a place that exists on the map, too often the setting enables the writer to excuse or rationalize its failures.

But what if we pay more attention to places that don't actually exist, at least not yet? This is exactly what George Saunders does in much of his fiction, and specifically, in his "Civilwarland in Bad Decline." Briefly, the story (from the collection of the same name) is set in a failing theme park called Civilwarland. The park is failing, in part, because it's being menaced by gangs from outside the park who terrorize both the paying customers and the employees in their period dress and who scare off potential investors to boot (the story begins as the founder of Burn 'n' Learn—a tan while you read business—considers investing in the park, until he sees gang graffiti where it shouldn't be). Simultaneously, the theme park is haunted by the ghostly McKinnon family, whose farm used to be where Civilwarland is now and who have their own awful, violent past to match the story's violent present. It is a pleasure to think of all the bad advice Saunders wouldn't have received for this story in a creative writing workshop: "My brother worked at Civilwarland for a summer, and it was nothing like this"; "The ghostly McKinnon family doesn't seem true to life to me"; "Would the founder of Burn 'n' Learn really speak this way?" etc. This is one of the wonderful things about Saunders's stories: they make many of the rules and distinctions regarding writing and the teaching of it seem beside the point. Don DeLillo has said that "realism is what we have agreed to call writing that actually has little connection to how we actually talk." This is certainly relevant to Saunders's fiction: he makes the notion of realism seem silly, but neither is he properly experimental or avant-garde. Better to think of his work, not in terms of realism, but in terms of plausibility, and plausibility is one of the most noble and most difficult achievements in fiction.

All of this is not to say that Saunders doesn't care about the setting of his story; indeed, he cares a great deal. Look, for instance, at the first sentence in "Civilwarland": "Whenever a potential big investor comes for the tour the first thing I do is take him out to the transplanted Erie Canal Lock." It is clear to anyone who sang "Fifteen Miles on the Erie Canal" in elementary school that this story is set in upstate New York—and those of us in the know will probably guess that Saunders is referring to the stranded piece of the old Erie Canal alongside the thruway between Rochester and Syracuse. We think this way, that is, until we read the rest of the paragraph: "We've got a good ninety feet of actual Canal out there and a well-researched dioramic of a coolie campsite. Were our faces ever red when we found out it was actually the Irish who built the Canal. We've got no budget to correct, so every fifteen minutes or so a device in the bunkhouse gives off the approximate aroma of an Oriental meal."

By the end of this paragraph, we should be disoriented, agreeably so. Where the hell are we, exactly? And how did we get here so quickly? These questions, of course, are precisely what Saunders wants to be asked: if we have firm sense of the Erie Canal, of upstate New York (if it's even in upstate New York; after all, it's never clear how far the piece of canal has been transplanted), then Saunders sets out to disturb it, to complicate it, to tear it down, and build it back up again. He wants to tear it down so that the reader can never be certain of his or her relation to the story, so the reader cannot be reassured by what the reader already knows (or thinks they know) about the characters, where they live, how they speak, etc. And he wants to build it up so that his characters and ideas and readers have a place to reside uncomfortably, so they might interrogate the discomfort.

The building it back up, of course, is the treacherous part, the part with which all writers have the most difficult time, and one of the reasons I admire Saunders so much is that he doesn't simply disturb our sense of place but brilliantly fashions the place itself. Saunders does this, to a great extent, through how he names things and his absolute fidelity to these names. Burn 'n' Learn, Historical Reconstruction Associate, Old Tyme Skills Seminars, Gift Acquisition Center, Dread Disease Rider, the Desperate Patrol, the Parade of Old Fashioned Conveyance, Revenue Impacting Event, and my favorite, the Verisimilitude Inspector—all of them capitalized, all of them mentioned repeatedly throughout the story. Saunders uses these laughably self-important titles and place names, in part, to satirize an insipid kind of middle-management speak that we should all recognize, that we hear constantly on television and from our too talkative neighbors, and that we sometimes hear coming out of our own mouths. But Saunders also uses these names to set the scene, to build the world of the story into a world that resembles the one with which we think we're familiar, but that is ultimately estranged from that real world. True, Saunders uses the above-mentioned inflated rhetoric to satirize our own degraded way of justifying our existence; but he also has perfect faith in his story and its worldview. He believes in his conceit, believes in his satire to such a degree that it becomes not a satire, or not just a satire, but rather a fully realized fictional world, estranged enough from our own that we can see ours clearly and we can also see ourselves in it clearly. Part of the difficulty in writing fiction is totally believing in what you've started writing, totally believing your story's warped vision of the world, its happily twisted logic, and then following that logic until it reaches its fullest dramatic extent. This is what makes Saunders such an inspiring model. It is not simply that the story is set in a place called Civilwarland, but that inside Civilwarland are the Cimarron Brothel, the Great Forest, Blacksmith Shoppe, and the Feinstein Memorial Conifer Grove. The names function the way the names on a map do when we are lost: the help orient us; or better yet, they let us know that we are disoriented. Badly so. This is true of the way the characters speak as well. Take, for instance, the scene in which the narrator and Mr. A. try to recruit an employee, Quinn, to fight off the gangs plaguing Civilwarland with live ammunition:

"The gangs in our park are a damn blight," Mr. A says. "I'm talking about meeting force with force. Something in it for you? Oh yes."

"I'd like to see Quinn give the rousing speech myself," I say.

"Societal order," Mr. A says. "Sustaining the lifeblood of this goddamned park we've all put so much of our hearts into."

"He's not just free associating," I say.

"I'm not sure I get it," Quinn says.

"What I'm suggesting is live ammo in your weapon only," Mr. A says. "Fire at your discretion. You see an unsavory intruder, you shoot at his feet. Just give him a scare. Nobody gets hurt. An additional two bills a week is what I'm talking."

"I'm an actor," Quinn says.

"Quinn's got kids," I say. "He knows the value of a buck."

"This is acting of the highest stripe," Mr. A says. "Act like a mercenary."

"Go for it on a trial basis," I say.

"I'm not sure I get it," Quinn says. "But jeez that's good money."

"Superfantastic," says Mr. A.

There is a great deal to learn from in this passage: the dialogue's fine literary misdirection alone is worth reading and rereading and mimicking, if necessary. But it's the riotous, cliché-ridden way of speaking that interests me at the moment: when Mr. A says "Superfantastic," Saunder's signals his character's identity and milieu the way other (sometimes lesser) writers use vernacular to convey a character's class and education and region. Writers often use this vernacular badly, because they have a too firm notion of what "real" people sound like—and they get this idea of what real people sound like not only from real life but also from hammy versions of the vernacular in bad stories or television shows or movies. But not Saunders—not when his characters speak, not when he lays out the geography of the park—and this is so because the story and its world are *his*; the story is not beholden to any preconceived sense of what people do or do not sound like in real life, because after all, what do people sound like in Civilwarland? In this way, Saunders's fiction does what Barthelme says all fiction should do: "art is always a meditation upon external reality rather than a representation of external reality or a jackleg attempt to 'be' external reality." The point, then, is not that the story is true to the real world, but true to itself, to its own carefully developed rules and logic—and in being true to itself, the story reveals more about the world than many supposedly realistic stories. Flannery O'Connor once said that "the writer has no rights at all except those he forges for himself in his own work." This is one of the most difficult things to learn as a writer—that no matter what rights we've earned in real life, no matter what our failures or triumphs, these rights and these triumphs and failures cannot be used to justify our fiction. This is why I teach "Civilwarland in Bad Decline": so students can see how Saunders achieves so much precisely because he doesn't assume that the difficult work in the story will have already been done in the culture it represents. My hope is that once students have learned this lesson and return to "real" places in their fiction, they will do so not so they can safely and endlessly mine the things they already know, but so they can do justice to the essential strangeness, the unknowability, the mystery that should have made them want to write about that place to begin with.

The Novel is Dead;
Long Live the Novel

It seems that every six months we're forced to endure yet another report on the Death of the Novel, or Failure of the Novel, or the Shrinking Audience for the Novel, or—conversely but not coincidentally—the Rise of Nonfiction. As such, we shouldn't be irked by these reports any more than we should be irked by the way, every six months, we're told to Fall Back or Spring Forward. We know every six months we're going to lose an hour we need, or gain one we don't, just as every six months we know we're going to be told that nonfiction is ascendant because it is timely and fiction obsolete because it isn't. At this late date in literary history, we know such an argument—always presented as though this claim is being made for the very first time and is Big News—is coming, and we should be ready for it, and be ready to ignore it.

But nevertheless, we are irked—irked because of the predictability of these reports; irked because they are written by people who know (or claim to know) what literature can do, who claim to be experts on the subject of Why People Read and Write Books, and yet who, somehow and repeatedly, completely miss the point that someone might go to nonfiction for one thing, to fiction for another. The problem is not that the different genres might do different things, serve different needs, have different goals, provoke different reactions in their readers; the problem is that by suggesting fiction should be more like nonfiction—*needs* to be more like nonfiction—both genres are badly diminished, and our literary world becomes a lesser place.

For an example of this kind of Sorry State of Fiction address, please consider Rachel Donadio's essay in the *New York Times Book Review*, "Truth Is Stronger Than Fiction." The title itself gives one pause, for what Donadio is talking about, of course, is not *truth* in a court-of-law or God sense, but about *books*—and what can it mean for a *book* to be strong? (One pictures the lamest booth at the fair, with novels struggling to raise the big hammer, to hit the lever, to ring the bell, while the muscular nonfiction books stand to the side in their strongman singlets, holding their already-won stuffed animals, flexing, asking the tube-topped girls passing by if they'd like to feel their biceps.) But really, there is nothing in Donadio's essay that we haven't read before; or to be more specific, nothing we didn't read twenty-eight years ago; or to be more specific, nothing that we didn't read in Tom Wolfe's 1989 essay "Stalking the Billion-Footed Beast," in which Wolfe demands that fiction writers write like Tom Wolfe, or else. Or else what? you might ask. A good, enduring question, it turns out, and the answer can be found in Donadio's essay: or else people will keep talking about the same subject in the same way using the same rhetoric until we figure out what exactly is being said, and why people keep saying it, and how we might get them to stop.

First off, it might be useful to know what it means to write like Tom Wolfe. It means to write a big realistic novel. We know this not just because this was the only kind of novel Tom Wolfe wrote (his four novels—*The Bonfire of the Vanities, A Man in Full, I Am Charlotte Simmons,* and *Back to Blood*—might not be inducted into the literary canon, but they certainly will be given a prominent place in the Doorstop Hall of Fame) but because he uses the phrase "big realistic novel" repeatedly in his essay, size being to Wolfe's essay what strength is to Donadio's. And as Wolfe makes clear, a writer needs to be big and strong because a *real* writer is more warrior than artist: "At this weak, pale, tabsecent moment in the history of American literature, we need a battalion, a brigade, of Zolas to head out into this wild, bizarre, unpredictable, Hog-stomping Baroque country of ours and reclaim it as literary property." According to Wolfe, once we have mounted our steeds, we should turn to journalists for our riding lessons: "The answer is not to leave the rude beast, the material, also known as the life around us, to the journalists, but to do what journalists do, or are supposed to do, which is to wrestle the beast and bring it to terms." Or, if there aren't any journalists on hand, we (meaning literary novelists—that is what I mean, and that is what Wolfe means as well) should look to writers of popular fiction, who "have one enormous advantage over their more literary confreres. They are not only willing to wrestle the beast; they actually love the battle."

The hilarity here is high (one imagines Wolfe in his famous white suit wrestling and defeating a beast—any beast will do—and one feels sorry for the poor beast, too, who no doubt entered the wrestling match thinking he was about to do battle with a mere *writer of literary fiction* and not *Tom Wolfe*), but to be fair, the metaphors of the hunt, the battle, are merely goofy and shouldn't concern us overmuch, except that essayists are still using them, and also still repeating Wolfe's dire warning from thirty-two years ago: "If fiction writers do not start facing the obvious, the literary history of the second half of the twentieth century will record that journalists not only took over the richness of American life as their domain, but also seized the high ground of literature itself."

The question of whether or not journalists "have seized the high ground of literature itself" aside, that verb—"seized"—is a significant one, in part because Donadio uses a similar verb in her essay. Her first sentence, for instance, aligns her with V. S. Naipaul in claiming that "nonfiction is better suited than fiction to *capture* the complexities of today's world" (emphasis mine). Later in the essay, Donadio repeats, "To date, no work of fiction has perfectly *captured* our historical moment . . ." (emphasis mine). What we're meant to learn here is that the very best literature doesn't evoke its subjects, or create them, or transform them, or render them, or distort them, or reinvent them, but rather "captures" them, as though they were enemy soldiers or Wolfe's beast. This is not so—in fact, the idea that fiction should *capture our historical moment* betrays a fundamental misunderstanding of what fiction can do to and with the world, and what the world does to it. But it is a useful misunderstanding, and we should be grateful for it, and for Donadio's use of *capture*, too: because if, as both Donadio and Wolfe claim, one of nonfiction's unique capabilities is to capture our historical moment (I have doubts this is so, but so many nonfiction writers insist upon it that I'm just going to go ahead and agree with them), then Donadio's use of the word lets us know precisely how far afield the tools and goals of nonfiction have led some novelists, and it also lets us see how important fiction is to our world and our imperfect understanding of it, even (especially) if fiction is never able to *capture* anything. Nor should we expect it to; nor should we *want* it to, except insofar as we'd like to live in a world simple enough to be captured.

For this is the point: we want literature to capture our troubled times, but our times are troubled, in part, because they are near impossible to capture. If our troubled times could be captured, would they be so troubled? In wanting our literature to capture our historical moment, we are asking, basically, for our literature to *simplify* our historical moment. When literature does so, the results are often disastrous. Take, for instance, Wolfe's own novels. Unlike his books of nonfiction—which are swift, funny, perceptive, curious, and which, to my mind, *evoke* and *transform* their times and places rather than *capture* their times and places—his novels are plodding, self-pleased, cartoonish. If Wolfe's nonfiction is about the hubristic tendencies of his subjects, his fiction tends to reveal more about the hubristic tendencies of its author. The trouble begins with Wolfe's conception of his books. This is his account of his 1987 novel *The Bonfire of the Vanities* in "Stalking the Billion-Footed Beast": "As I saw it, such a book should be a novel of the city." Later, he describes the same novel as "a big book about New York." Bigness is part of these novels' problems: it is not just that they are long, but that they are flabby, turgid, gasbaggy: Wolfe no doubt intended them to be full of life; instead they seem full of Wolfe.

But really, it is not mostly that the novels are overlong: it is that they set out to be the final word on a subject—New York and the 1980s in *The Bonfire of the Vanities*, the New South and the 1990s in *A Man in Full*. Wolfe's prepositions—"of" and "about"—are significant, in that they tell us the author does indeed want to capture his complicated subjects, to stand for them, to exhaust them. The problem is, his subjects (class, race, regional identity, municipal and national politics) *are* complicated, and as such they refuse to be captured unless, of course, you make the make them less complicated. Wolfe's characters—whether they are Black or white, rich or poor, southern or northern, new southern or old southern—must be reduced to exactly these categories, these types, these caricatures, if Wolfe is going to capture them. One's historical moment is more easily understood this way, of course; but then it also becomes an historical moment not much worth understanding.

Take Wolfe's approach to New York itself at the beginning of *The Bonfire of the Vanities*. The Jewish mayor of New York is holding a press conference in Harlem in which he is shouted down by the mostly Black crowd, and after briefly attempting to verbally spar with the crowd, the mayor (and the novel) retreats to this internal monologue: "Come down from your swell co-ops, your general partners and merger lawyers! It's the Third World down there! Puerto Ricans, West Indians, Haitians, Dominicans, Cubans, Colombians, Hondurans, Koreans, Chinese, Thais, Vietnamese, Ecuadorians, Panamanians, Filipinos, Albanians, Senegalese, and Afro-Americans!" Wolfe means for this list to convey how New York is spiraling out of (white) control, but instead the passage is oddly tame and generic, as though it were written by an excitable census taker. Everything about the rhetoric ("swell co-ops"; "general partners and merger lawyers") speaks not of chaos but of categories, of generalities. As Wolfe unintentionally shows us, chaos is specific, but control is generic. This is also true of Wolfe's subsequent account of New York's neighborhoods:

> Morningside Heights, St. Nicholas Park, Washington Heights, Fort Tyron—*por qué pagar más!*—The Bronx—the Bronx is finished for you! Riverdale is just a little freeport up there. Pelham Parkway—keep the corridor open to Westchester! Brooklyn—*your* Brooklyn is no more! Brooklyn Heights, Park Slope—little Hong Kongs, that's all! And Queens! Jackson Heights, Elmhurst, Hollis, Jamaica, Ozone Park—whose is it? Do you know? And where does that leave Ridgewood, Bayside, and Forest Hills? Have you ever thought about that? And Staten Island!

Again, Wolfe means for this list to convey something about the big demographic changes in New York in the 1980s, about how alive and terrifying he finds the city, but the passage comes off as something narrated by a highly pessimistic real estate agent: a reader who doesn't know New York won't know it any better at the end of the list; a reader who does know New York, or thinks they know it, won't have any better or different understanding of the city at the end of the list, either. What does Wolfe think he's doing, then? Wolfe's own account—again in "Stalking the Billion-Footed Beast"—of his attempt to capture this chaos is telling: "The past three decades have been decades of tremendous and at times convulsive social changes, especially in large cities, and the tide of the fourth great wave of immigration has made the picture seem all the more chaotic, random, and discontinuous." If this is true, then why do the above-quoted passages from *The Bonfire of the Vanities* seem about as random and chaotic as a roll call? Wolfe, again, provides the answer: "The economy with which realistic fiction can bring the many currents of a city together in a single, fairly simple story was something I found exhilarating." The author might indeed find it exhilarating to be able to take a complicated story and make it simple, but as readers, we should not be so thrilled, unless, of course (as Donadio suggests), we want fiction to *capture* our chaotic times, and to organize it and reduce it in the process.

Wolfe's approach to the city is similar to the way he approaches his main characters. Briefly, the novel (told in omniscient narration) focuses on married investment banker Sherman McCoy, who is having an affair with Maria, a wealthy southerner married to an older man; Larry Kramer, a somewhat down-on-his-luck Jewish lawyer working in the DA's office; and an expatriate British journalist, Peter Fallow. Early in the novel, Sherman and Maria find themselves in a bad neighborhood in the Bronx, and, panicking, Maria (who is driving Sherman's car) runs over and kills one of two Black boys Maria and Sherman think are about to rob them. Inevitably, then, this act brings McCoy closer and closer to Fallow—who reports on the (as yet) unsolved hit-and-run—and Kramer, who will be involved in prosecuting the case.

As Wolfe himself would say, this story is "fairly simple," as is the way Wolfe defines his characters. Sherman is known from the novel's beginning as "Master of the Universe"; Maria, aside from her physical attributes, is known by the way she pronounces Sherman's name ("Shuhhh-mun"); Kramer is known by his self-loathing, his unrealized dreams ("Let's face it!" Wolfe screams at his character early on, "... You're an American workdaddy now! Nothing more.");

Fallow, who is by far the most interesting character in the novel if only because Wolfe must feel an obligation to his fellow journalists not to reduce them to mere types, is known by a number of ways, but mostly by his inebriation.

There is nothing inherently wrong with these characters, or with the way Wolfe initially defines them. After all, one must never approach one's characters through character summary. Instead, as Donald Barthelme says, "The world enters the work as it enters our ordinary lives, not as worldview or system but in sharp particularity." True, Wolfe sets up his characters in a somewhat dubious, simplistic fashion: Sherman is set up to fall, Fallow to rise, Kramer to stay more or less where he is. And it is also true that limitations of the characters—the way they see themselves and their worlds, the way they're reduced to types and they way they reduce themselves to types—indicates something about their creator's own limited sense of the world and its inhabitants. But all that aside, it could be said that Wolfe does what all novelists do: he finds an economical way to introduce his characters ("Shuhhh-mun"). And after that has been accomplished, the novelist must give them the sort depth, mystery, and complexity (through dialogue, internal monologue, point of view, metaphor) that their real life counterparts might not exhibit, and that nonfiction thus might not be able to report on.

But Wolfe is not able to give his characters this depth, or at least he chooses not to, and that is due, in part, to his training as a nonfiction writer. For instance, nearly halfway through the book, Sherman reads a newspaper report (written by Fallow) on the Black teenager—Henry Lamb—whom Maria has run over with Sherman's car. The report doesn't name him, but clearly someone will, soon, and clearly the article portends bad things for Sherman:

Our pity is not good enough for Henry Lamb and the many other good people who are determined to beat the odds in the less affluent sections of our city. They need to know that their hopes and dreams are important to the future of all New York. We call for an aggressive investigation of every angle of the Lamb case.

Basically, this article tells Sherman his life as "Master of the Universe" is over, and his life as a known philanderer, racist, and felon is just beginning. And what is Sherman's reaction? "He was rocked." Wait: Is that it? What can this mean: *He was rocked*? It is so generic as to mean nothing. On one level, *of course* he was rocked: who wouldn't be? But Sherman should be defined by his reaction to this sort of terrible news; we should get some sort of specific, startling insight into his character, something that will elevate him beyond the caricature he has thus far been. How, exactly, is he rocked? What are the particular manifestations and properties of his rockedness? Wolfe doesn't say, and why not? One could argue that Wolfe is lazy: after all, it's difficult to really look into a person, to try to fathom or at least imagine their inner life, their mystery, which is why, in real life, we choose not to do so all the time. But I don't think Wolfe is merely lazy; I think Wolfe's training as a journalist—precisely the thing he says the contemporary novel needs—is what prevents him from writing the novel he wants to write. After all, if McCoy were a real person, and Wolfe were writing a nonfiction piece about him, he would not be able to say what McCoy was thinking. And unless Wolfe was there while McCoy was reading this newspaper article, he would not be able to see McCoy's visible reaction, either. As such, in a piece of journalism, the sentence "He was rocked" might not seem so lacking (in fact, at the end of the novel, there is a newspaper article on Sherman that reads, "Mr. McCoy's marriage was rocked by the revelation...." and, as a piece of journalism, the description seems not nearly as lazy as it did when "rocked" was the sum and total of Sherman's point of view). So, using his background as a journalist, Wolfe has Sherman be rocked—and later on, after Sherman tells his wife, Judy, about what he's done, "She was staggered"—and then escapes before things get difficult, before he has to give his protagonist a meaningful point of view, an inner life. But these things *are* what a novelist can do, should do, *must* do: a novelist has the opportunity to look inside, to imagine a person's depths, and a novelist must take advantage of that opportunity. Wolfe believes in width (as when he casts his wide net and hauls in the names of New York's neighborhoods and nationalities), but a novel is not a novel because it spreads wide, rather because it goes deep (there has to be a better way to say that), just as a novel is not a novel because it captures our troubled times, but because it illuminates and imagines the specific aspects of the trouble.

If a writer must give his characters an inner life—a unique way of seeing the world and themselves—if they are to help make a novel a novel, then a writer also must also give characters their own particular way of *talking* about the world. But again, Wolfe's experience as a journalist inhibits his characters speech. Sherman is Wolfe's primary character and therefore the primary example of Wolfe's limitations. Two thirds of the way through the novel, Sherman is about to be arraigned for his crime, and he tries to tell his six-year-old daughter how he'll be mentioned in the newspapers and on television and to not believe what she hears.

"Will you be in history, Daddy?"

History? "No, I won't be in history, Campbell. But I'll be smeared, vilified, dragged through the mud."

He knew she wouldn't understand a word of it.

Of course Campbell doesn't understand a word of it, any more than she would understand it if her daddy had told her he was rocked. Campbell doesn't understand what her father is saying, not because she is six years old, but because her father isn't saying anything that would make her (or us) *want* to understand him. Sherman speaks in clichés, and he speaks in clichés—Wolfe would later explain—because real people speak in clichés. This is a truism, I suppose, because we've all used clichés and we're all real people, or at least, we want to be; and, as Wolfe understands it, a realistic novel has its characters speak the way real people speak. Again, if Wolfe were writing a nonfiction piece about Sherman, and if Sherman spoke in clichés, then Wolfe couldn't very well have him speak otherwise. But this to my mind is a limitation of nonfiction, not a strength, and when applied to fiction it becomes a liability. After all, the novelist can have his characters speak in a way they might not be able to, or want to, in real life. This is not to say that the novelist should make them sound implausible, but if he could make them speak in way that defines them, that transforms, elevates, degrades, and in any case, *deepens* their sense of themselves, and our sense of them, then why would he choose not to? Why would Wolfe choose, in the novel's opening scene, to have the crowd respond to the Mayor in this fashion: "*Go on home!... Booooo ... Yaggggghhh ... Yo!*" Whether a crowd might respond this way in real life is important to Wolfe—one can picture him sitting in the back of the crowd, tape recorder in hand, an urban anthropologist in white bucks recording the speech patterns of the natives—but if he's writing a novel, it should not be the most important thing. After all, how does the "*Boooo*" distinguish this crowd from a generic crowd? And if it doesn't, why bother having them say it? Did Wolfe's experience as a journalist suggest that he add a fifth *g* in "*Yagggggghhh*"? And why oh why that "*Yo!*"? Did Wolfe really believe he nailed the Black vernacular by the "*Yo!*"? If this is realistic dialogue, why would we want a novel to employ it? After scenes like this, we almost long for Sherman's clichés, until we hear them again, as in this scene, in which Sherman responds to his impending arrest in the following canned fashion: "I can't believe what I've done. If I had only played it straight with [Maria]! Me!—with my pretensions of respectability and propriety!" One could argue, of course, that this passage just shows Sherman's limitations, but all of Wolfe's characters speak in ways that prevent insight and merely propel the book from one high-pitched, over-the-top scene to the next. As such, the way Sherman speaks points not to a failure of language, but to a failure of Wolfe.

I'm not saying here that every journalist is doomed to write bad novels, or that fiction is superior to nonfiction, or that realism is inferior to whatever we choose to label its opposite, but if one is going to write a novel, then one had best emphasize and pursue its virtues as fiction, and not try and make the novel more like nonfiction. Wolfe admits that "One very obvious matter I had not reckoned with: in nonfiction you are very conveniently provided with the setting and the characters and the plot. You now have the task—and it is a huge one—of bringing it all alive as convincingly as the best of realistic fiction. But you don't have to concoct the story. Indeed, you can't. I found the sudden freedom of fiction intimidating." Wolfe's solution, then, was to apply the rules of nonfiction to fiction as a way of abdicating the freedom (*freedom* being a well-known euphemism for *difficulty*) of writing a novel. This involved Wolfe creating a doppelgänger, as he acknowledges in this passage: "Like most journalists who have been handed a story, Fallow was eager to persuade himself that he had discovered and breathed life into this clay itself." Rather than breathe life into the clay, however, Wolfe assumes the clay already has a life of its own, and all he has to do (to hopelessly mix the metaphor) is to slap the clay down on the page and call it a day, and a novel. And the clay, in this case, is New York of the 1980s—an important, complicated, unpredictable time and place, to be sure, though you wouldn't know that from *The Bonfire of the Vanities*.

Wolfe is to blame for the quality of his own books, of course, but so are we as readers: we tend to think important novels are important because they are *about* or *of* something inherently significant. For instance, we often talk about F. Scott Fitzgerald's *The Great Gatsby* as being a great novel *about* or *of* the Roaring '20s, as though the novel were important only because it's about an important historical moment. True, *The Great Gatsby* uses its beautifully wrought, memorable characters to evoke its historical moment. But it is not *about* the Roaring '20s the way Wolfe says his novel is about New York; it does not *capture* the Roaring '20s the way Donadio seems to suggest great fiction should (and, at the moment, doesn't) capture our own historical moment. When we think of the Roaring '20s, we might think of *The Great Gatsby,* not because we know the era but because we know the book. This is a testament to the greatness of the novel, not to its choice in subjects. But we would not know the novel— or want to know it—so well if it set out to be about the era instead of about Jay Gatsby, Nick Carraway, and Daisy and Tom Buchanan.

I am not suggesting, however, that the novel is incapable of engaging with our historical moment, and that it should only look inward, or that it should look outward but only in the most ethereal, exalted way possible. Indeed, the only thing more irksome than the semiannual Death of the Novel report is the defense that fiction may not chronicle current events, but it does chronicle more important things—like the Human Condition, or even worse, the Human Spirit. The gushy imprecision of these terms make one want to fall back into the big strong arms of nonfiction. Donadio suggests that this is exactly why contemporary readers and publishers are more invested in nonfiction than fiction: "Fiction may still be one escape of choice—along with television and movies and video games and iPods—but when it comes to illuminating today's world most vividly, then nonfiction is winning." But are these our only choices: books that provide an escape from our historical moment, and books that set out to capture and thus (I would argue) simplify our historical moment? Shouldn't we get more than two choices?

We should, and we do, though one wouldn't get that impression from Donadio's essay. As her essay would have us understand it, after September 11, 2001, there are nonfiction books that have tackled our historical moment, and novels that have avoided the contact: "If, as Naipaul argues, fiction is no longer adequate to make sense of the world, then it's understandable why magazines and readers turn to nonfiction. As a rule, novelists shouldn't become editorialists, but it's safe to say no novels have yet engaged with the post–Sept. 11 era." It is not safe to say this. There *are* novels that have engaged with the post–Sept. 11 era. The problem here is more Donadio's *idea* of the novel than the novels themselves. When she writes that "no novels have yet engaged with the post–Sept. 11 era," she means that there are no novels like the kind Wolfe has written—big realistic novels that attempt to *capture* or *make sense of* the post–Sept. 11 era. As I hope I've shown, we should not want those kinds novels as badly as we've been told we should want them. But that aside, there *are* novels that have represented this era in its difficulty, in its absurdity and tragedy. These novels have not pretended to capture or make sense of our era, which is precisely why they're worthy and why we should read them.

The best example of such a novel is Heidi Julavits's 2003 *The Effect of Living Backwards*. Briefly, the book is about a group of airplane hijackers who may or may not actually be hijackers, and two women (Alice—who is the novel's narrator—and her soon-to-be married sister, Edith) on the airplane who may or may not be complicit in their own hijacking (if it is one), and something called the International Institute for Terrorist Studies, whose mission is either to prevent terrorism or promote terrorism, or perhaps both, and which is either behind the plane hijacking, or trying to stop it, or perhaps both. It should be clear from this too brief synopsis that instead of capturing and making sense of our world—as Donadio seems to think literature should do—Julavits creates a stylized, surreal, but not-unrecognizable version of our world, a world that evokes our own world's confusions and contradictions without attempting to be a replica of it.

In other words, *The Effect of Living Backwards* is the antithesis of *The Bonfire of the Vanities*. Early on in the novel—which is nonlinear and which begins near the book's chronological end—the Institute asks Alice what it asks all it students: "But how can you be so certain?" This is not a question Wolfe would ever ask, given that he believes novels must "wrestle the beast and bring it to terms." But Julavits recognizes that this is very much a novelist's question: a novel cannot broach difficult subjects and still be a novel without asking itself and its characters, "But how can you be so certain?" Wolfe suggests a novelist must have the authority of a reporter; in contrast, Julavits suggests authority is a euphemism for a lack of curiosity, and that if an author is going to do justice to her subjects, than she must be curious about them, all the while admitting that if they are truly complex, then there is no way for an author to capture them. A novelist can gesture toward and evoke a subject's mystery but cannot pretend to solve it. Alice's account of Bruno, the (possibly) blind head hijacker—"Something about the guy bothered me. He seemed too confident of his puzzle place in the greater interlocking world"—is telling, and what it tells us is that in our post–Sept. 11 era, we should be wary of people who seem too certain of themselves, and we should be equally wary of books that seem too certain about their subjects, and of critics who want them to be.

This sense of uncertainty (which, I would argue, is kissing cousin to curiosity) is what makes *The Effect of Living Backwards* such an important novel—in part because it believes in its own fictiveness, believes that as fiction it can do something that nonfiction cannot, and in the process it shows us exactly how Wolfe's novel fails as a novel and how we should not keep asking for novels to repeat that failure. Take, for instance, Julavits's approach to dialogue in the book—specifically, to the way people of different cultures and nationalities speak to and understand each other. The stakes are high, because Julavits is trying to evoke a world that's defined by a person from one culture's inability to understand a person from another, a world in which one may hear one's enemies issue threats in a language one doesn't understand, and so one hears the threats not directly from the threateners but rather from those who translate the threats. What to do, then, as a novelist? Wolfe would argue that a novelist must write the dialogue as a reporter would, and one must do so with authority and accuracy (*"Yo!"*). But Julavits suggests otherwise, as in this scene when Alice is asked to speak with a hostage negotiator who "pretends to speak only in Sasak," a language Alice also speaks, but not well.

> *"Snamo?"* a voice said. *"Gno mnabo nay?"*
>
> *"Snamo,"* I responded.
>
> *"Gno mnabo nay?"* the man repeated...
>
> "I am Alice," I replied. My Sasak, never exemplary, was pretty rusty. "We have been hijacked."
>
> There was a pause.
>
> "Your Sasak is barely adequate..."
>
> "My apologies," I said, disconcerted, "it's been a few years." (Literally I said, "Look away from this sorry girl, many years until Sasak talking.") "Barely adequate" was more than polite assessment. My Sasak sucked...
>
> "And yourself, Alice, you are well?"
>
> "I am a wallet head of exuberance," I told him in Sasak.

The first thing to be noted about this scene is that it is very funny. The humor comes, in part, from Alice's lack of authority: she barely knows what she's doing, and this is funny because in her situation we wouldn't know what we'd be doing, either. In other words, the author doesn't give her narrator an implausible command of a strange and difficult situation, and this helps the reader empathize, whereas the authority of reportage would keep the reader at a distance. Moreover, the imprecision of Alice's translation—and the other hijackees' dependence on it—reminds us that in our attempt to understand the world, we're also dependent on someone else's possible imprecision. But the scene is also funny because funny is exactly what we don't expect a novel about an airplane hijacking to be. After all, immediately after September 11, we were told by nearly anyone with a microphone or a computer that funny was no longer an option, at least as far as certain subjects were concerned (airplane hijacking presumably being one of them). How does Julavits get away with it? In part, she does so by not worrying about whether she's going to get away with it or not, but also by having the negotiator and Alice speak in a language (it's spoken on the island of Lombok in Indonesia) so obscure that most readers will wonder if it even exists, thus allowing the reader a distance, a perspective, that the reader wouldn't have if they were speaking, say, Arabic. In other words, Julavits never forgets that she is writing fiction, and this is what fiction can do with our historical moment: it can provide us a vantage point from which we can look at our moment, and thus can give us insight into our moment that the real world (and the people who report on it) cannot provide.

The Effect of Living Backwards also succeeds because of the way it treats its sources. As I've already demonstrated, Wolfe demands that a novelist go out and act like a reporter, which is to say, report on what he sees and hears, what he witnesses. Donadio tacitly agrees with this, and suggests that nonfiction writers have surpassed fiction writers because they are more willing to report on real life, to talk about reality. But both Donadio and Wolfe have a ruinously narrow view of real life: by real life, Wolfe and Donadio mean something that one has witnessed "in the field," and then perhaps augmented by archival or historical research to support what one has witnessed. But is that all real life means? Fortunately, for a fiction writer, that is not all it means. Yes, novelists care about what they witness, and they also care about history, fact, verisimilitude; but those are not the only things they care about. Flannery O'Connor once said that "the writer is initially set going by literature more than by life." I would amend this slightly and argue that literature is one of the things *in* life that sets a writer going, which is another way of saying that literature isn't something artificially added to life or extraneous to life, but part of it. But the idea that when we talk about life we also talk about literature—and, I would add, art and culture—has been lost, and it is clear why: what we regard as real life is so confusing that we need to get rid of everything else (literature, for instance) so that it might become something less confusing. For instance, as Benjamin Kunkel puts it in another *New York Times Book Review* essay, it was commonly thought and opined immediately after 9/11 that "literature . . . couldn't matter much at first, in the face of so much murder and alarm." It is true that, after the World Trade Center was destroyed, no one was walking around demanding people get reacquainted with the Great Books. But isn't it also true that when we saw the airplanes plow into the towers, part of our response to that terrible sight was our memory of similar scenes in books, movies, visual art of all kind? When we saw Osama bin Laden on television, did we see only Osama bin Laden, or did we also see the terrorists in Don DeLillo's excellent 1991 novel *Mao II*, or for that matter, the terrorists in Arnold Schwarzenegger's and James Cameron's loathsome 1994 movie *True Lies*? Of course we did, for better or worse. And this is why we want to make the world smaller, more cramped; this is why some of us want to *not* think of art and literature when we think about the world: it is difficult enough to understand bin Laden and our response to bin Laden without also thinking about how art has influenced our response. But fortunately, this is what fiction can do: it can restore the world to its full complication, whether the world wants it to or not. Consider, for example, this terrific moment in *The Effect of Living Backwards* in which Alice and Edith argue about their hijackers:

> "There is something very, very strange about all this," I said. "Something's not right about this hijacking."
>
> "And you would know, being such the veteran."
>
> I frowned. "So where are the police, Edith?"
>
> "Napping," she said. "Selling arms to children. God knows. This is Africa, Alice. The police might be worse than the terrorists."
>
> "Where are the reporters?"
>
> "Filing their stories, I guess. Where do you get these expectations? The movies?"
>
> I stared at her as if to reply, *Where does one get one's ideas about anything?*

How much more terrifying and exhilarating the world seems after this scene! How much bigger the world seems when we ask ourselves the question, *Where does one get one's ideas about anything?* This is what the novel does, after all: it makes us see our many sources for understanding the world, and in the process makes the world seem bigger, even if we don't want it to be. Which is why we then call for novels like *The Bonfire of the Vanities*, which makes our largest, most vibrant city seem about as expansive and dangerous as Sioux Falls on a Sunday night.

Of course, the bigger the world gets, the more confusing it is, and *The Effect of Living Backwards* doesn't attempt to downplay the confusion, as Julavits shows through hijacked plane's pilot's announcement: "[The pilot] apologized for unlocking the cockpit door—but how could we blame him? How was he to know that a steward was a hijacker? What had happened to trust in this world? Why wasn't anyone who he was supposed to be anymore?" I should say that the confusion in the novel is a confusion not of the nihilistic, there-is-no-such-thing-as-the-truth confusion but a confusion that very much evokes our historical moment's confusion, so much so that the book's characters wonder if the simplest answer might not be, in fact, the right one. (As Alice tells another passenger, "We can't rule out the possibility that this is a good old-fashioned hijacking.") Nor are we, as readers, allowed the comfort of knowing that the simplest answer is the true one. In fact, one of the most terrifying things about *The Effect of Living Backwards* is that it gives us *various* plausible answers to our most important questions, answers that are based on distorted but recognizable versions of our own experience, as when one of the passengers asks Bruno, "Why can't you just act normally?... Why can't you just shoot people or fly us into a building?" After Bruno considers this question, he replies: "Because, Justin... that would make me a common terrorist."

At this juncture I should pointed out that nowhere does Julavits say her novel is *about* September 11, though it clearly evokes September 11, and it clearly depends on the reader's memory and experience of September 11 (for instance, it refers to a previous disaster as The Big Terrible, which, by the way, is also what *New York Times* columnist Thomas Friedman called September 11). And while the passenger asks Bruno why he doesn't "fly us into a building," that is the only time such an act is mentioned, and there is no scene in which we see planes crashing into the World Trade Center. This absence is significant. It might be true that nonfiction profits by approaching its subjects directly, but this is not true of fiction: after all, by *making up* its characters (even if they're based on something or someone in real life), fiction automatically approaches its subjects indirectly, by virtue of its fictiveness. Though Donadio and Wolfe view this as a drawback, Julavits's novel shows us otherwise: if the Big Terrible is really so terrible, then it defies our attempts to completely understand it, to make sense of it, to *report* on it with authority, to approach it head on. All one has to do is read Jonathan Safran Foer's cloying and deeply unsatisfying novel *Extremely Loud & Incredibly Close* to see the perils in approaching The Big Terrible directly. Instead, as Julavits makes clear, we might best take on such massive subjects in ways that might not exactly comfort us, but are surprising, irreverent, provocative, entertaining, and edifying. As Alice herself states, "We *imagine* we will react a certain way to imminent tragedy, and yet the reality is that the mind fails to respond as we expect it will respond." Donadio claims that nonfiction is best at responding to our times, but I would argue that fiction—through its uncertainty and curiosity, its sense of invention and mystery—is our most powerful reaction to tragedy, our most enduring document of how we think we're going to respond to it, and how we actually respond. In *The Effect of Living Backwards*, Julavits doesn't make sense of our historical moment the way, say, Friedman tries to in his nonfiction book *Longitudes and Attitudes: The World in the Age of Terror-*

ism, but she does something more difficult and more rewarding: she shows the chaos, the *lack* of sense, of the post-9/11 era. In *The Effect of Living Backwards*, one of the hijackees tells Alice that the world is odd, and Alice responds, "'The world isn't that odd . . . The world tends to make a lot of sad sense.' I didn't actually believe this." Fifty years from now, people will read this passage and be able to learn a great deal about the confusion of our time, will understand how little sense it made, and will also understand something about our thwarted desire to *make* it make sense. They will not necessarily get this impression from Friedman's book, no matter how timely it is. This is another way of saying I'm willing to bet that in fifty years we will still be reading Julavits book, but we won't be reading Friedman's. That's not because Friedman's isn't worth rereading; rather that between now and 2056, some other nonfiction book will come along, something more timely than Friedman's book, and someone will be saying how sad it is that fiction isn't as timely as nonfiction anymore, how it doesn't capture the era, and if we're lucky, novels like Julavits's will still be around to show us how fiction doesn't have to capture an era to engage it, and how we, the readers, shouldn't want it to in the first place.

The Imagined Life

Fiction does a lot of different things to a lot of different people, but it's recently become clear that one of the things it does to some of those people is make them *nervous*. This was obvious in the wake of 9/11, when you couldn't spit (I tried) without hitting someone proclaiming that fiction didn't and couldn't matter anymore. And it was obvious when David Shields published his 2010 book *Reality Hunger*, in which he claimed "I doubt very much that I'm the only person finding it more and more difficult to want to read or write novels." And it was obvious when my son brought home these helpful definitions from his third grade teacher: Fiction: Books or Stories That Are Not True, Like Make-Believe or Fantasy Stories. Nonfiction: Books or Stories That Are True and Real. They Teach and Inform Us. Because this is what people do when they're nervous: they try to declare dead, or dismiss, or define away, the things that made them so nervous in the first place.

On one level: good. I'm glad fiction makes people nervous, especially hand-wringing opportunists who use The Day We Will Never

Forget or their own self-aggrandizing manifestos as excuse to declare postmortem on an art form that they'd probably (and resentfully) never found alive in the first place. Fiction *should* make them, and everyone else, nervous. I knew a guy—one of the most intelligent, enthusiastic readers of modern fiction I've ever met—who, while reading, had the odd (and dexterous) habit of biting his fingernails and then storing the gnawed slivers and shards in his shirt pocket, as though to enjoy them later, or to use them to remember and appreciate what made him nervous back when he'd bitten them. This is an excellent, albeit disgusting, metaphor for what it can be like to read fiction, and why so many of us love it, even (especially) when it makes us so nervous.

But on another level, this nervousness is troubling, especially when it causes people who love fiction to praise it backhandedly. This is true of my son's third grade teacher, for instance, who, despite her gerrymandering distinction between fiction and nonfiction, was a bigger fan of the former than the latter. And it's also true of some of our best book reviewers. Take, for instance, Liesl Schillinger's March 13, 2001, *New York Times* review of Tea Obreht's novel *The Tiger's Wife*. Schillinger is one of my favorite reviewers—a smart reader, eloquent writer, and impassioned advocate for books she deems worthy of advocacy. And she loved Obreht's novel. But look at the way she expresses her love: "Téa Obreht was born in Belgrade in 1985 but left at the age of 7, before the major conflict took hold. . . . In other words, she did not live in the former Yugoslavia during the war-torn years this book revisits. Filled with astonishing immediacy and presence, fleshed out with detail that seems firsthand, *The Tiger's Wife* is all the more remarkable for being the product not of observation but of imagination."

With all due respect to Schillinger (and to Obreht, whose book I haven't read), it is not more remarkable that the novel is good for being a product of imagination and not observation. It is not remarkable at all, except insofar as all novels that manage to be good are remarkable. After all, this is what novels are supposed to do: they're supposed to imagine a world into existence. And this is what novels (and their reviewers) are *not* supposed to do: confuse observation with insight, autobiography with art. I know that Schillinger is trying to do justice to Obreht's achievement, but is the way to do that to diminish the whole fictional enterprise, to suggest that, admirable aberrations like *The Tiger's Wife* aside, most great novels manage to be great because they *don't* rely on imagination?

Likewise, consider Laura Miller February 6, 2011, *Salon* review of Kevin Brockmeier's *The Illumination*. Miller is a terrific reviewer, and like her, I loved *The Illumination*, which, as Miller puts it, "begins on a day when, all across the globe, people in pain begin to glow." But she is missing the point when she writes, "Brockmeier's consistently arresting observations have the throb of lived—rather than merely imagined—experience." Maybe Miller's lived experience is more exciting than mine, but I doubt it. I doubt her life, or Brockmeier's, is any more *throbbing* than anyone else's. To put it bluntly, lived live stinks, aesthetically speaking, for all of us; we are usually too busy living it to actually imagine what form it might take, what it might mean. In other words, we are *merely* living it; whereas Brockmeier's imagination—well, there is nothing "mere" about it. This is why we need novels like Brockmeier's: not because they are based on, or can replicate the feeling of, lived experience, but because they can do better than that. They can take something overwhelmingly grim—like 9/11, for instance—and imagine paths into and out of it in ways they couldn't if they were relying only on experience and observation.

All of this is to say that we shouldn't be so nervous and defensive while talking and writing about fiction. Maybe we should even take some cues from reviewers of nonfiction. *New York Times*'s Michiko Kakutani, for instance, named James Kaplan's biography of Frank Sinatra—*Frank: The Voice*—one of her ten books of 2010 and claimed it was a "biography that reads like a novel." Like a novel! I hope Mr. Kaplan takes this as a compliment. And if he doesn't, well, it makes me nervous to think that a good fiction reviewer wouldn't be able to tell him why he should.

Let Me Tell You What It Means to Be from Upstate New York: A Loser's Love Song

Let me tell you about something that happened twenty years ago in a laundromat in Rochester, New York. The laundromat was on Park Avenue. Park Avenue in Rochester is to Rochester what Park Avenue in Manhattan is to Manhattan: it has nice shops and restaurants; it has beautiful homes full of handsome, well-scrubbed white people. Unlike Manhattan's Park Avenue, it has a laundromat. Two decades ago, outside the laundromat, it was snowing, because it always snows in upstate New York. Inside the laundromat I was taking my clothes out of the washer and putting them into the dryer. A pair of my ratty boxer shorts fell on the floor, which was slushy from everyone's boots. I threw the boxer shorts in the dryer anyway. I didn't have a job, and I hadn't had a job for a long time, and it seemed possible that I would never have a job again. This should have made me sad, but it didn't, mostly. Because I was in the laundromat in the middle of a weekday and the laundromat was full of unemployed losers like me, and so I knew I wasn't alone. There was a table next to the dryer. The table was there to fold your clothes on, or to dump your quarters on and then count them, hoping that *this* time you would actually have enough coins to fully dry your clothes. The table closest to my dryer was occupied, but not by clothes or coins: two women were using it to talk over. These were the kind of people who treat every public space like a coffee shop. They had placed their enormous metallic travel coffee mugs on the table and were conversing loudly and hurriedly in an obviously overcaffienated way. This was in the dark years before everyone owned enormous metallic travel coffee mugs, and maybe that's why the women seemed exotic to me, like they probably weren't from the area. Or maybe they seemed that way because of what I heard them say.

"I hate this place. I'm moving to Ithaca," one of them said to the other (Ithaca, two hours southeast of Rochester, is home to Cornell University, Ithaca College, and the famous vegetarian restaurant The Moosewood; it is the undisputed upstate New York capital of political right-mindedness). "As soon as possible."

"I *love* Ithaca," the other woman said.

"I know," the first woman said. "Ithaca is an oasis of liberalism in a sea of rednecks."

Like a lot of upstate New Yorkers, I'm defensive about upstate New York, even though I'm not an upstate New York native, and even though I loathed upstate New York for at least half of the twenty-seven years I actually lived there. My family moved to Little Falls (halfway between Albany and Syracuse) from Massachusetts when I was three. I never felt at home in Little Falls, not once in the fifteen years I lived there before going off to college in Pennsylvania.

I know now I wouldn't have felt at home anywhere, that I was an enormously self-involved, self-pitying baby, no less so at three years of age than at eighteen, no less at eighteen than at forty. But I didn't know that then. All I knew was that I didn't feel at home, and so I blamed Little Falls, the fact that I *lived* there but wasn't *from* there. Frederick Exley, in *A Fan's Notes*, describes Glacial Falls (a fictional town near the real Watertown, which is to say so far north that you can't believe there's more New York before you get to Canada, except there is—hours of it) as "a rural community of ten thousand, buried half the year under leaden skies and heavy snows, and all the year under the weight of its large and intransigent ignorance." That's the way I felt about Little Falls, except Little Falls had barely more than five thousand citizens, and so was only half as big as Glacial Falls, and so it had to be twice as bad, even though Glacial Falls wasn't even a real town and I hadn't even read Exley's book yet. By the time I did read it, I had begun to fall in love with upstate New York, and with Little Falls, but before then, I wanted nothing to do with the place. When someone asked me where I was from, I usually said Springfield, Massachusetts, where I had been born and where my middle brother had been born and where my mother had been born and where much of my extended family still lived. Sometimes, I said I was from Boston, where my favorite sports times played and where I imagined living someday. I never said I was from upstate New York until I got the hell out of there and went to college.

This might be a good time to discuss what is meant by "upstate New York." People are famously cranky on this subject. For some ridiculous people, upstate New York is anything north and west of Westchester County in southern New York; for other, slightly less ridiculous people, it's everything north and west of the Tappan Zee

Bridge; for more reasonable natives, it's everything north of Interstate 90 (which basically cuts New York into north and south halves). For my father, there is no such thing as "upstate New York": according to him, he lives in central New York, whereas people in Buffalo and Rochester live in western New York, people in Jamestown the Southern Tier, people in the Adirondacks the Adirondacks, and so on. For him, the term *upstate New York* is a media (in other words, New York City) contrivance, and thus means nothing at all; for others it means everything. A lot of the people (like me) who belong in the latter category seem to be writers. Percival Everett in his novel *Erasure* diagnoses and satirizes this particular writerly illness by having a character-who-is-a-writer say in a biographical note that she is "a resident of upstate New York" to which the novel's narrator comments parenthetically, "(apparently all of it)."

It should be said that this is part of what it means to be from upstate New York: to presume to stand and speak for an entire region, and then to define the region in a way designed to exclude as many people as possible who think they already live in it, on top of the self-exclusion of the millions of New Yorkers who have no desire to live in it in the first place. But anyway, this argument about what is meant by upstate New York has gone on long enough, so let me settle it once and for all by saying this: when we talk about upstate New York, we really mean my hometown, Little Falls.

Let me tell you a bit more about Little Falls.

It's small: that much you already know. Even when it was big, it was small. In 1920, it had 13,029 citizens. As of 2000, it had 5,188.

It exists, mostly, on the north side of the Mohawk River and Erie Canal, though there is some Little Falls left on the south side, too. When I was growing up the south side was an Italian neighborhood;

it still is, somewhat, though the rest of the white people (Little Falls is 97.78% white) let the Italians cross the river now.

When I grew up there, there were three Roman Catholic churches: St. Mary's (which was the Irish church), St. Joseph's (Italian), and Sacred Heart (Polish). There were and are Protestant churches, too, but I know nothing about them, or about most of the people who attend them, or even what it's like to be Protestant, even though my father is one, or at least his parents were. My mother is Italian, but she and my brothers and I went to St. Mary's, the Irish church, maybe because she was new to the area and didn't know any better, or maybe because St. Mary's, with its soaring spires, was by far the most beautiful of the three churches. Anyway, now there's just one remaining Roman Catholic church. It's St. Mary's, except now they call it Holy Family—appealing, I guess, to the new sense of inclusiveness that also allows the Italians to cross the river to join the rest of their Little Fallsians.

Speaking of the river: the city exists because of it. Which is to say the mills and factories that used to employ so many Little Fallsians would have existed elsewhere if they didn't have to river as power source, the river as trash receptacle, the river (and, once it was built in 1825, the Erie Canal, which also runs through the city, in places in confluence with the river) as transportation. And without the mills and factories, there wouldn't be a Little Falls—at least not in the way most Little Fallsians and I think of it. Little Falls would be mostly farms, though there are far fewer of them than there used to be. There are far fewer mills and factories than there used to be, too (during its industrial heyday, Little Falls factories made, among other things, shoes, paper, boxes, bicycles, Union Army uniforms, cheese, milking machines, and starch), for which the river is no doubt grateful. The people who used to work in those factories and mills aren't so grateful. A bunch of those people have moved away from Little Falls and from upstate New York to find work—mostly, it seems, to Charlotte, North Carolina. The story of late twentieth century north-to-south migration is an overfamiliar one, and so I won't go into it, except to say that if someone were looking to start a Little Falls now, they probably wouldn't choose Little Falls to do it. If someone hadn't been looking to start a Little Falls a long time ago, there probably wouldn't be a Little Falls now. But there was, and there is.

Let me tell you about the first time I realized I might be in love with Little Falls.

I was in college—the end of my senior year. It was the middle of May. I'd just graduated and was preparing to go home, for the summer, and maybe even longer. I wasn't thinking about it as something to dread or something to look forward to: going home for the summer was simply something you did because you had to. It's probably the same feeling some Americans had when they'd been drafted to serve in the military. I was packing my bags when my roommate came in. I'd stolen a lot of his clothes during the school year (by which I mean I'd worn his clothes without asking him if I could and then, like a sartorial squatter, acted like they were rightfully and legally mine because I was wearing them), and he knew it (knew it because, of course, he'd seen me wearing his clothes) and said, "Let me see what you've packed."

"Why?"

"*Why?*" he said in disbelief. "Because I don't want any of my clothes going back with you to Little Falls."

Then my roommate started digging through my bags, and I let him. Because I wasn't thinking about my—or rather, his—clothes anymore. Because the words *Little Falls* had given me an odd feeling. It was a feeling somewhere between exhilaration and doom. It was like the feeling you get when you hear a *boom* somewhere off in the distance.

"Jesus Christ, Brock," he said, and started yanking his clothes out of my bags and stuffing them in his own.

"Sorry," I said, but I wasn't, really. I was too busy thinking about Little Falls. I could picture Main Street, which the natives called "downstreet," (as in, "I'm going downstreet tonight") which was equal parts old-fashioned main drag and dollar store; I could picture the old factories and shacks clinging to the banks of the river as it roars and rumbles by until it joins with the Erie Canal and becomes more peaceful and navigable; I could picture, just north of the river/canal, the tin pole barn fiberglass plant in which I worked the summer before, and, during our half-hour lunch, where I chugged beer in the parking lot with the rest of the guys—guys for whom this wasn't a summer job but the best job they'd probably ever have—before going back into the plant, where I sanded fiberglass shells and itched and itched and itched; I could picture standing, drunk, in the parking lot and looking south, out at the cliffs that mark the beginning of the long climb out of the Mohawk Valley and toward the Catskill Mountains; I could picture standing, drunk, in the parking lot and looking north, out at the buildings—the grand Masonic temple, the prosaic Stewart's convenience store, the old Rialto Theatre that was about to complete its inexorable journey from *Drums Along the Mohawk* through *Deep Throat* to demolition, the stately Victorian and

Federal style homes surrounding Western Park—on the hill above downstreet that marked the beginning of the short climb north out of the Valley, past my parents' house and toward the Adirondacks. Even though it was May, I could picture winter: I could picture me as a teenager lying in bed at five in the morning, listening to the wind howling, warning me to stay the hell in bed; I could hear my father's snowblower growling, warning me to get the hell out of bed; I could hear the *crack* of someone driving through the sawhorses the city put at the top of our road to indicate that it was closed, still closed, because of the snow that the plows couldn't clear fast enough. I could picture myself in that car. The car was saying, "Good-bye, goodbye," and I wanted to say that, too. I'd always wanted to say that to Little Falls. Except now I didn't anymore, and why not? My roommate's clothes were going home with him to Westchester County, but I was going home to Little Falls to find out.

When I describe Little Falls to people who've never been there, they say, "It sounds like a Richard Russo novel." They're right: it does. Because it is. Russo grew up in Gloversville, a slightly larger factory town thirty minutes to the north and east of Little Falls, and many of his great books are set in upstate New York towns resembling Gloversville (and Little Falls). It's no surprise, then, that when I talk about Little Falls, I sound like I'm talking about a Russo novel; it's no surprise, then, that when I read one of Russo's novels, I think of Little Falls. But I also think of Little Falls when I read Russell Banks's *The Sweet Hereafter*, which is set in the even smaller towns in the northeast part of the Adirondacks; when I read William Kennedy's *Ironweed*, which is set in Albany, the state's capital seventy miles east of Little Falls; when I read Exley's *A Fan's Notes*, which is set in Watertown, a much bigger, much snowier, much more rugged town than Little Falls. This is not to say that all books set in upstate New York are alike, but that all great books, no matter where they're set, make you love people, places, and things that, in real life, would be and are difficult to love.

Let me tell you what happened the summer I moved home after college.

I tried to, as that terrible song tells us to do, accentuate the positive. I dumped my bags in my childhood bedroom and walked outside, determined to see Little Falls in a way I hadn't before. I stood on my parents' deck and took note of the lovely green, green hills rising south out of the Valley; my father was standing next to me, and I told him that I never realized how *beautiful* the view was, how the hills were maybe the most beautiful hills *I had ever seen*. My rhapsodizing about the sublime seemed to unnerve him; he mumbled something about it being time for dinner and walked back into the house, where dinner was waiting for us. I followed him. Dinner that night was chicken wings, which we'd picked up from a pizza place downstreet on the way home. Chicken wings, as everyone knows, are to upstate New York what pasta is to Italy, the gyro to Greece, vodka to Russia, Peking duck to Peking: you can get them everywhere, but nowhere are they as good as they are in upstate New York. I shared this theory with my parents at dinner: how the wings I'd had while at college in Pennsylvania were nowhere near as good as these wings, how these wings were *perfect*. Positive overstatement is looked down upon in my family—it's like talking about your medical problems, or your relationship problems, or your financial problems, which are also looked down upon—and so, to change the subject, my mother began talking about one of Little Falls's well-known drunks, who was also a well-known cop, and how finally the city had had enough of the guy being a well-known drunk while being on duty as a well-known copy, and fired him. Which prompted the now ex-cop to get even drunker than usual one night and dump sugar in the gas tanks of all the unattended cop cars he could find until a cop caught him in the act and threatened, not to arrest him, but to call his wife, which put an end to the crime spree. My mother's tone while telling this story was one of bemused disapproval, but my tone in responding to it was one of hysterical appreciation. I told my mother that this was what I'd been telling my college friends: that Little Falls cops were the most crooked, drunk cops in the history of crooked, drunk, small-town cops and that they were employed to protect and serve the quirkiest of citizens and how *hilarious* Little Falls was. My parents didn't say anything to that at first. My father looked down, balefully, into his mostly empty Dixie cup of blue cheese; my mother stared at me in a concerned way, and then finally said, "It's not so bad."

Suddenly, I felt sick; the feeling had nothing to do with the chicken wings I'd eaten. It's the sickness you feel when you lie to yourself. Because to accentuate the positive requires one to lie to oneself. When my mother said, "It's not so bad," the lie was dismissed and the truth reintroduced. The truth was that the Valley was pretty, all right, very pretty, but I knew there were prettier views in the world, and for that matter in the state, and for that matter in the same county; the truth was that the cops in Little Falls weren't any different than other cops in other small towns, and its citizens weren't any quirkier than any other small town citizens; the truth was that the chicken wings were delicious and better than chicken wings elsewhere, but they were *just chicken wings,* for chrissake.

"I'm going to bed," I told my parents. I did. I slept for twelve hours. Then I got out of bed, the bad taste of the lie still in my mouth, and looked around again, and found Little Falls to be as dull and depressing as ever. I remembered the way I'd felt when my roommate had said "Little Falls," but now that I was actually there, I didn't feel the same. This, like unemployment (I didn't have a job and hadn't acquired the proper skills in college that might have made me qualified for a job), was another post-college disappointment: college changed the way one thought about the real world, but the real world didn't necessarily change to match the way one thought about it in college.

A week after I'd moved back home, I mentioned to my father this theory and how it applied to Little Falls, and in response, my father didn't ignore me; he didn't tell me to stop being such a self-pitying baby. Instead, he gave me a book to read (my father was an English professor at the local community college): it was Russo's second novel, *The Risk Pool*. I read it, then read Russo's first novel *Mohawk*, and then read all of the other books I mentioned earlier. And then, when I was done, I read them again. When I was through with my reading and rereading, I looked once again at Little Falls. And finally, I felt about the place the way I'd felt when my roommate had said its name. It was reading the novels that had done it. It wasn't that they made me realize what I'd thought grim was actually beautiful. They had not accentuated the positive. Rather, they had made something beautiful out of something grim—beautiful not because the people magically became less poor, or became noble in their poverty; beautiful not because the towns became less decrepit, or noble in their decrepitude; beautiful because the towns were physically—by which I mean naturally—beautiful, and that beauty somehow conspired with the towns' decrepitude to make the former less pristine, the latter less hopeless; beautiful because the towns kept on trying to fight their decrepitude, the townspeople their poverty—sometimes with grace and good humor, sometimes with bitterness and lies. But always fighting the notion that these places and these people didn't matter. Sometimes that notion came from without, and sometimes from within, but the characters didn't stop fighting against it, and neither did the novelists, all the while recognizing that the fight was probably already lost. What was beautiful was not some bullshit sense of inner beauty, not some romantic post-industrial, post-Wordsworthian sense of the sublime appeal of abandoned, rusting silos and paper mills; what was beautiful was that the novels had made something surprising and artful out of compromised materials. It was like eating the most unpromising part of an animal (the wing of a chicken, for instance) and actually *liking* it, because you knew no one was else would. Even though you knew no one else would.

That's why I was furious at the women at the laundromat twenty years ago, the woman who said that she hated Rochester and that Ithaca was an oasis of liberalism in a sea of rednecks and the woman who agreed with her. I wanted to ask them if they knew how lucky they were to be in Rochester, and not Syracuse, or Utica, or, God forbid, Binghamton (because this is also what it means to be from upstate New York: to thank whatever God you believe in that you don't live in another, worse, town in upstate New York). Did they not know how lonely it made me feel to hear them bad-mouth the place I loved? Did they not know it made me think there was something wrong with me for loving it? Did they not wonder, just for a second, that maybe there was something wrong, not with Rochester, but with them? I wanted to tell them something about Rochester that would change their minds about it. I wanted to tell them, for instance, that Rochester had the second largest gay population, percentage wise, in the country, after San Francisco. But mostly I wanted to tell them that Ithaca might be an *island* of liberalism in a *sea* of rednecks; or it might be an *oasis* of liberalism in a *desert* of rednecks. But it could not be an *oasis* in a *sea*. An oasis, I wanted to tell them, needs sand. But was that even true? After all, what did I know about the desert; I had never seen one. At that point, I'd lived most of my life in upstate New York. And for that matter, I wasn't really sure that Rochester really had the second largest gay population in the country, either. Some random guy had told me that—in the very same laundromat, in fact—but I had no proof, no statistics. So I didn't say anything. I kept my mouth shut, hating myself for keeping my mouth shut. But I did get my petty little revenge. I closed the door to the dryer, walked over to the table, dug into my pockets and dumped my change right onto the table, startling the women, who lifted their coffee mugs. "*Excuse* me," one of them said. "No, excuse *me*," I said, and then leaned over the table, and started to count the quarters, hoping I'd have enough.

Acknowledgments

These essays first appeared in the following magazines, anthologies, and newspapers (sometimes in significantly different form): *The Believer, The Boston Globe, The Chronicle of Higher Education, The Cincinnati Review, Lithub, The Rumpus, The Writer's Chronicle, Virginia Quarterly Review, My Word* (Sarabande Books), and *Why We're Here* (Colgate University Press). Thanks to all the editors of those publications, especially Nicole Lamy.

Thanks to Nicola Mason—my editor, and friend—for giving this book a chance, and the right title, and such a good home.

Thanks to my colleagues and students at Bowdoin College.

Thanks to my family, who first appeared in my life, and then in these essays (sometimes in significantly different form).

Finally, infinite thanks to these people: Jess Anthony, Sara Corbett, Pete Coviello, Erica Dawson, Michael Griffith, Heidi Julavits, Kevin Moffett, Keith Morris, Jason Ockert, Jeff Parker, Mike Paterniti, Lewis Robinson, Richard Russo, Trent Stewart, Justin Tussing, Corinna Vallianatos, and Caki Wilkinson.